# Separately

# Together

*The Key to Understanding your Relationship*

## DR MARTIN SPURIN

Illustrations by Isabella Snow

Matador
9 Priory Business Park,
Wistow Road, Kibworth Beauchamp,
Leicestershire. LE8 0RX
Tel: 0116 279 2299
Email: books@troubador.co.uk
Web: www.troubador.co.uk/matador
Twitter: @matadorbooks

ISBN 978 1785892 189

British Library Cataloguing in Publication Data.
A catalogue record for this book is available from the British Library.

Printed and bound in the UK by TJ International, Padstow, Cornwall
Typeset in 11pt Aldine401 BT by Troubador Publishing Ltd, Leicester, UK

Matador is an imprint of Troubador Publishing Ltd

# Separately Together

For Sarah.

# Foreword

Unless the decision is made for us, at some point we choose to live with our partner. It's so exciting early on to think of being with that one person every day, but the excitement can wear off. Sometimes it takes years to notice the change, sometimes it's just a matter of weeks. The longer it goes on, the more restrictions we have regarding choices, to the point where we do not have any real option but to stay with our chosen one. It's not easy living with someone; in fact, it can be incredibly hard – even if you like them.

It can be difficult enough just looking after ourselves, because being human isn't easy at times. It doesn't matter what age we are, we're never fully equipped to handle some of the problems that come our way. Life can take us in directions we didn't plan for and down roads we didn't want to go. We can often wonder how on earth we got ourselves into the position we're in. Most of us do strive for happiness, but we don't always recognise it when we're there. If you think back on your life, there might have been times when you thought you were really happy, but it's only afterward that you realise it. Very often it's only when we have something to compare it to that determines whether it was good or not. In the same way, it's only when we compare ourselves and our relationship with those around us that we can establish the normality of our own lives.

*…you've wondered what life would be like if he snuffed it on the way home from work…*

What most of us seem to have in common is this desire to find someone to share our life with, but it rarely seems to work out how we thought it would. The dreams we had of living happily ever after and having a family seem more like hard work now. The longer you live with someone the more you find out how different they are from you. *Why does he think so differently? Why is he always so …? How come he never seems to …? Why is sex so …? Do I really want this?* If you want to improve things, you need to understand not only how your partner thinks, but also assess what your own needs are. Stripping down the common beliefs about relationships and love will help you to do this. That's where this book comes in.

## What's it all about?

Essentially, this book is about examining heterosexual relationships. It is fundamentally about you and your relationship with your partner. But how do you establish whether your relationship is normal for a start? Do you really want it to be? When we observe other relationships it might make us think that we probably don't want the same sort of relationship compared to the majority. The book focuses on developing an understanding of yourself and where you are now with your partner, in order for you to find ways to improve it – if that's what you want. This, in-turn, should help you to be more aware of yourself and the part you play in that relationship. The book also gives you an insight about the way he thinks and how, with this understanding, you can start to get more satisfaction. As you read, keep in mind that the quotes are a very important part of the book.

Later in the book, I discuss sensitive issues such as sex. I know this is very intimate and personal in our lives (although there are always those who seem quite happy to tell us all the gory details of what they get up to), but it's an important element in a relationship. Yet, a lot of women don't really enjoy it and a lot of men don't do it.

You might be in a relationship that, at times just feels awkward. Perhaps the intimacy has gone. It may be the case that one or both of you don't really put much effort into it as you're so used to each other. There's an expression for this: 'you don't need to run after the bus once you've caught it'. That might be you. It might be that you spend more time not being together. You may even be at a point where you've wondered what life would be like if he snuffed it on the way home from work (although deep down you wouldn't actually like that to happen – but you have thought it).

Maybe it's just that he takes you for granted. You do everything around the house. The only things you don't clean are his teeth. Are you at the stage where those little quirks that you ignored in the beginning are really niggling you now? The way he forcefully and proudly releases air from various parts of his body as if they need to hear it next door, the way he always speaks for you when you're with others, the fact that he can't take his vest off without an anaesthetic or the annoyance that his boobs are now bigger than yours. Perhaps you've just realised that the squeak you keep hearing in bed isn't actually the bed after all – it's him. You might feel the relationship is not right, but you don't want to lose him. You believe in the old saying: 'A husband is for life – not just for Christmas'. After all, he is yours. More than likely he's only ever had one previous owner and that was his mother.

If things don't feel right in a relationship, they tend not to be right in the bedroom. Are you at a stage where you are trying to cure him of any intimate physical ambitions? Are you wearing nighties that, quite frankly, would scare burglars? Sex now seems more like a ritual (if you have it at all); something you wouldn't call an enjoyable experience. You just go through the motions or, worse still, simply feel cold when he touches you.

NOT THE NIGHTIE WITH THE BARBED WIRE AGAIN!

On the other hand, it might be that you want to have a close intimate relationship, but you're making love, on average, less than residents at the local care home. It might be that he's just not interested. Or, perhaps, he never times it right when he has a pee, so everything fizzles out just when it's getting interesting. For a man timing his pee before sex can take a lot of planning. He can't go when it's up and he can't do it when it's down. You never know whether he's coming or going. Also, for men the orgasm is never quite as good if he's dying for a pee. That's the problem with a multi-purpose appliance: there's such a lot of planning involved.

It might be the case that you're young and starting out in a relationship, but you're not sure whether you're going to like sex or not. You've read *Fifty Shades of Grey* and feel it went rather well for her in the book, but you're not so sure if you're going to feel the same. It may be that those around you seem to be having more fun than you and so you assume that something is wrong with you. It might be that you've tried having sex but you can't see what all the fuss is about; you seem to have more fun watching party political broadcasts whilst defrosting the freezer.

There are all sorts of reasons for reading this book. Perhaps you just sense things are not right for you. It might be that you've felt this for some time or that you've only just realised it. You might only realise there are problems once you've finished reading this book. We can go for years without confronting issues or confiding in someone as it can be difficult to admit truths when we've never even admitted them to ourselves. It might be that you would like a greater understanding of relationships and why they end up like they do. Alternatively, it could be that you just want to understand why men think and act the way they do. To accommodate these various motives the book is in two parts. Ingeniously, I call them Part One and Part Two – quite a good idea, I thought.

## Part One

The first section is about having a foundation of understanding about relationships. It starts by looking at the concept we have of what is normal – about ourselves and our relationship. I explain that it's an unconscious assessment that we make every day of our lives, but only consciously ask it when we're forced to, very often after a relationship has broken down. It's often only when things go wrong in our lives and we reflect on our own life that we are more in tune with ourselves. However, trying to make sense of it is difficult and the idea of confiding in someone seems complicated for some reason. Something is stopping us really telling someone our innermost thoughts and feelings, but why? Well, they might think we're not normal for a start. You may feel that you couldn't talk to someone else about it because you wouldn't know what to say, probably because you're not even sure at times how you feel – let alone what you want to do about it. Also, who can you confide in? Who do you know that you can trust? I address this in the first chapter as I talk about how you may be feeling and why you may be sceptical about talking to someone. Is there anyone who would listen to you – I mean really listen?

In chapter two, I go into the difficulty of actually talking to each other and the worse possible things you can ever say to a man. I identify the reasons for marriage and explain how romance in books and films can give us a misguided ideal about love and being in love. I ask the question 'how do you know how you feel about someone?' And if you don't know, I offer you a technique to help. This leads on to defining what *love* is and why the concept of being *in love* is different, as well as being so temporary. Here I introduce the concept of separately together as I explore what constitutes a healthy love as opposed to an unhealthy one, which might surprise you. Then, I explain how it is so easy for intimacy to drift, *especially* when children come along.

In chapter three, I look at how those in a relationship can drift off into having an affair and why it turns out to be very different from the fantasy. It's a complicated activity because we're often talking about satisfying human needs. We all have these needs and when they're not fulfilled with our partner we can often look elsewhere to get them attended to.

At the core of this book is the understanding of ourselves and our relationship. Therefore, in order to make that assessment, having some understanding of how you chose your partner and why communication often breaks down within it is important to know. In chapter four, I suggest that our choice is often determined by our upbringing. I explain how we deal with stages of development and how these may influence our behaviour as an adult. This not only affects the relationship we have with our partner, but is also instrumental in choosing that particular person, hopefully to spend the rest of our lives with. Here, I try to offer an explanation as to why you behave as you do and how this determines whether communication works or not with you and your partner. It also explains how you are with others in your life.

*He needs training …*

## Part Two

It could be that you just want to know more about how your man (or men in general) thinks. It's only by having this understanding that you can begin to do anything about him. You may want some practical ideas of what to do, or you may want him to have some idea about how you are different and how you don't have the same attitude towards things as he does. This is where the second part of the book comes in.

You might have heard that men think about sex all the time, but what exactly is going on in their minds? What do men find attractive? Find out in chapter five. Here, I reveal a secret about something you wear which has absolutely no impact on men because they never notice. I tell you something quite unusual about how your man sees your body that you may have never noticed. I introduce the concept of individual fantasies and how everyone has them, even during sex. I also explain why men's personalities change when they are with their mates.

Men generally won't read this book (unless they're nosey and want to see what you're reading, just in case they need to be prepared), so if it's the physical side of things you want to focus on then look at chapter six. Here, I look at what you need to do to improve life in the bedroom (and I don't mean changing the curtains or clearing up that nasty stain in the corner that's been there for years). Unfortunately, in the bedroom, you can't rely on him to work things out for himself, not if you would like some sort of satisfaction. He needs training, or retraining, and that's where you will have to take the lead. But, before you do any training or start telling him what you want him to do for you, there is something very important you have to know first.

I'll tell you in chapter six. While you're there, I'll explain how he learns about sex and why he is desperate for more guidance.

Some men don't have sex, or just can't get it up. It might be that sex is an awkward subject for you both now, so you don't even go there. Therefore, in chapter seven, I look at impotence and the reasons for this. I give you an example of a couple from literature and how they overcame their difficulties to give you some ideas to try, if this is a problem in your relationship. I'm not going to go into the medical side of all this or tell you to use certain products. It's just all about showing you another approach to benefit your relationship.

Although this book is essentially written for women, chapters eight and nine aim to offer men suggestions about how to go about things in the bedroom, as well as outside it, as part of his training. 'It's strange that so many of us find it easier to have sex than to talk to each other' (Godson 2011, p21). So, if you're not fulfilled in the bedroom and not in a position to talk about it with him, you might want to think about getting your partner to read these two chapters at some point if you can, after you've read them yourself, of course! Here, I identify how his approach might be a bit of a passion killer – from underwear to his technique. I explain why couples don't really know what each other likes in the bedroom and why neither can ask. I then try to give ideas about creating the right atmosphere and conditions for developing the sensual side of love-making. If you find telling your partner what you like in bed difficult, I suggest something you could introduce to overcome this.

In chapter nine, I give some thought about how he can satisfy you *outside* the bedroom. I explain the scoring system women use when it comes to receiving gifts and I give examples about little things he could do which could mean a lot. The main aim of chapters eight and nine is to ensure he knows how to make you feel loved and cherished.

If you do manage to get him to read chapters eight and nine, then he might consider reading other chapters, such as chapter ten, and this might give him more of an understanding about why women can go off sex. This will, at least, make him think about what you have to go through as a woman and why the heavenly parts of your body he dreams of are not thought about in quite the same way by you. It might make him think that he needs to be a bit more considerate, patient and gentle with you. I also talk about the stereotypical woman's role in the family and how her identity can be swamped and mislaid while she's busy looking after everyone else.

*Ignorance can be bliss; it works for so many people.*

## Deep down – we really know what's best

Once, an old farmer, tinkering with a rusty harrow on a country road, was approached by an earnest young man… who was making farm-to-farm calls for the purpose of selling a new manual on soil conservation and new farming techniques. After a polite and polished speech the young man asked the farmer if he would like to buy this new book, to which the old man replied:

'Son, I don't farm half as good as I know how already.'

Harris 1973, p4

This little story from Thomas A. Harris, the American psychiatrist and author of the best-selling book 'I'm OK, You're OK', tells us, that deep down we know how to live our life properly, it's just that we choose not to. We know that smoking will probably eventually kills us horribly, we know that drinking too much is bad for our health, we know that eating the wrong type of food isn't good for our body – but we still do it. We know what's right for us, but we choose to ignore it. The problem is that many of us then look for someone to blame when it all goes wrong. It's the same with relationships. That's the great thing about marriage – there's always someone there to blame instead of us. A lot of us don't look inwardly and when it comes to our relationship we can convince ourselves that we are happy. It might stem from us not wanting to confront issues for fear of what we might find. Either way it can take a lot of energy.

Unfortunately, if you want to rectify or improve a relationship, or even have a better sex life, there's not a pill you can take that will instantaneously improve everything (which is a shame really, because there seems to be pills for almost everything else). Problems, generally, don't just go away. Therefore, you have a choice: you either put up with the situation, which means that you might moan a lot about it, or you do something about it.

What I try to do in this book is get you to think about your circumstances a little bit differently. O'Connor and Seymour (1993), specialists in neuro-linguistic programming: an approach to personal development and communication, advise that if something doesn't work for you then you need to try something different. If you always get the same results, then you need to do something very different. On the other hand, it might just be a case that you perhaps want to understand yourself more, or at least be more aware of where you are in your relationship. The problem with this is that awareness can bring you pain. And once you are aware of something you can't go back to the way you were before. It's a bit like me saying to you: 'don't think of an elephant'. What do you think of? You can't go back to being ignorant and forget what you now realise. Ignorance can be bliss – it works for so many people. It may just simply be that you want to understand what men are like and how their minds work. I must point out that I do over-generalise in this book, so when I talk about men keep in mind it may not be all men – just all the ones I know.

COMING SOON FROM YOUR PHARMACY

DOSAGE PER DAY
1 TABLET PER DAY = SOLVES YOUR PROBLEMS
2 TABLETS PER DAY = HAPPINESS
3 TABLETS PER DAY = DELERIOUS

# Chapter One

*Are you normal? Is your relationship normal? Who do you talk to when you feel things aren't normal?*

In this chapter I cover:
- Why relationships establish whether we're normal.
- The conscious and unconscious assessment we make.
- The concerns we have when confiding in someone.
- Finding someone who really does listen to us.
- What the signs are that indicate something is wrong in our relationship.

*…loneliness is often more difficult to cope with when you're actually living with someone.*

The question: 'are you normal?' is a strange one – a question that we only tend to consciously ask ourselves when we recognise that things are not right in our life. Most of the time we don't think about it, but it is one that we assess unconsciously all the time. How we do that is by interaction with other people and forming relationships. I must point out here that we don't know exactly what *normal* is, but we have a good idea about what we find unacceptable and outside the parameters of what we consider normal. For example, when we read about violent murderers or paedophiles we just know that they don't fall within the parameters of normal. Therefore, we sort of have things that are acceptable to us and things that aren't. Normal tends to be what the majority of people do (or don't do).

You may have heard of Abraham Maslow, the American psychologist and originator of the hierarchy of needs. It's a very famous, easily accessible, theory that most students will have studied by the time they leave university. The general understanding of the hierarchy is that as one level of needs gets satisfied, we move on to the next level. In the middle of the hierarchy is the category of 'social needs': the need to feel we fit in and belong. It's this that is at the core of our need for relationships. Relationships help us to feel normal. We may only have a small circle of friends, we can't really like and be close to everyone, and we tend to gravitate towards those who share our beliefs and values as this confirms our own view on the world. At the same time we're interested in what significant people have to say. We're interested in people's lives, their opinions and what they eat for tea. We live in a celebrity society where we get bombarded with what people are doing in their relationships. Biographies and autobiographies of famous people are popular. We want to know how they think and then we unconsciously compare it to how we think. We get into characters in soaps and books and then become intrigued by the relationships they have and how they deal with life. It is this that gives us the opportunity to compare our beliefs and our thinking with others. It is this that helps us to feel that we are a *normal* member of society, having the same sorts of problems as anyone else. This is where we unconsciously assess the answer to the question 'am I normal?' We can only do this by comparing the way we think with others.

The need to understand where we fit in with other humans extends to the friendships that we form, and especially one relationship in particular. Seeking a close loving relationship with someone is important to us at some point in our lives and central to our being. We even fantasise about it, especially when we're with the wrong person. This one relationship is an integral part of our make-up. We have hopes and dreams of sharing our life with someone else and being happy with them as that seems to be the human existence plan. It's what has happened in history, it's what happens around us and it's what happens in books and films. Therefore, throughout our life, we have the belief that there is someone suitable out there for us to be happy with. That's why there are so many online dating agencies. They appeal to our intrigue of finding the right person.

The ultimate result of finding the right person is very often marriage, or, at least, living together. That's what we do. It's what most people do. As a society, and entrenched in many religions, we come to believe in marriage and it's a very happy event when one takes place. Unfortunately, they don't always work out. In fact, there's a very good chance that they won't. However, when they don't work out, people don't lose hope or the belief in the arrangement so they often have another go. There is a strong inner belief that intimate relationships work and that we need them. That's why when a marriage isn't going the way we want it to we often turn to someone else. We like to feel love and we want to share our love with someone who appreciates it.

The majority of novels and films contain a strong social element as a central theme. The two main characters, usually male and female, good looking and about the same age, have been apart throughout the film or antagonistic toward each other, but they've got to get together by the end – that's the rule, that's what we expect. If they don't, we feel a bit cheated somehow – it's the final piece in the jigsaw, they can now live together happily ever after.

The social need, as identified in Maslow's hierarchy, is an important element and it is this that helps us determine and establish whether we're a *normal* member of society. In this way, we have unconscious, unstated guidelines as humans that we tend to follow without thinking. As this is often shaped by our upbringing, we then construct a world that confirms our beliefs and expectations and act accordingly.

You might feel quite normal yourself. It's quite easy to convince ourselves most of the time because we tend to circulate with others who confirm this for us. Obviously, how we evaluate ourselves is very important, but being with someone else in a relationship is not so easy. In fact, it's really hard. Relationships evolve over time and all of a sudden you can realise that it's changed quite a lot.

Do you have the feeling that not everything is quite right in your relationship? The relationship may not have been right for some time, but we've not recognised it until now. It seems quite normal compared to other couples, but is that enough? Perhaps you sense things have changed and you're not feeling the way that you used to towards your partner. If so, when do you think things started to change or go wrong? If you've narrowed it down to just after the wedding reception then there's a lot of work to do and I'm not sure all the answers you're looking for are in this book. The need to talk to someone about the situation may have reached a critical point because, essentially, the relationship we have with our partner is the foundation that supports everything else we do.

Unfortunately, you may not be quite certain yourself about how you feel, let alone be ready to confide in someone. Yet dealing with it in isolation can dominate your mind. It can feel lonely in a relationship and the problem is that loneliness is often more difficult to cope with when you're actually living with someone. It can be much easier dealing with it when you're living on your own. However, most of us want a normal relationship and deep down we have hope that our partner wants us and that our relationship can be happy.

*No one quite knows what's going on inside of you …*

## Someone to talk to

You may have thought about talking to someone, but that in itself is associated with lots of issues. Within each relationship we are a slightly different person because we adapt to the personality of the other. You'll have friends who you wouldn't dream of telling certain things to. You might choose one person for one thing and another for something else, even though they might be a closer friend to you. For some of your friends, it's just not worth telling them anything. They just wouldn't get it. They might get it for a bit, but 'whenever I find someone who understands a *part* of me at the time, then it never fails that a point is reached where I know they're *not* understanding me again' (Rogers 1967, p53). No one quite knows what's going on inside of you and no one can fully appreciate or understand what you're going through, simply because everyone is different. We all have different relationships and therefore have contrasting experiences and interpretations. However, we're quite well aware of who we can confide in. If we want our secrets spread around, we all know someone who can do that for us. Every place of work seems to employ at least one person specifically for this purpose.

One problem when confiding in someone else is that, very often, if they get upset you have to then deal with them and their emotions. I remember telling a friend of mine that my marriage had broken up. I told him a few months later and he ended up getting upset with me because I hadn't contacted him at the time. I then had to deal with his emotions when the situation wasn't about him – it was about me. This confirmed to me just why I didn't tell him in the first place. We adapt our behaviour so that when we know someone might get upset, it's just easier not to tell them, it's a natural and therefore normal reaction.

## The art of listening

Sometimes you're not sure how you feel. People can often assume what you mean and then tell you what's best for you, without really listening or knowing who you truly are. How many people do you know who genuinely listen to you and make you feel that you're the most important person in the world at that moment? How many people do you know who look you in the eyes as if they're searching your innermost feelings and hanging on to every word? My guess is that you'd struggle to identify three. At the same time you need to think about how you are with others.

Do you consider yourself to be a good listener? Think about your close friends and try to appreciate what their world is really like, what they have to deal with, and what worries they have. You might feel you know, but actually this might just be your own assumption. If you come to the conclusion that you don't really know your friends, it may indicate that you don't really ask them searching questions or genuinely listen to them. They might just consider you to be someone who simply ends up telling them what they should do.

Would you get upset if a friend of yours talked to someone else instead of to you? If so, this may imply jealousy on your part, which perhaps stems from your own insecurity. It may indicate that you want some sort of control over the relationship and have expectations over their behaviour. Whereas, if you truly cared for them, you would be pleased that they have someone to talk to, because when you really care for someone it often means letting go and not putting conditions on them. They may have concerns about telling you something. Is your behaviour consistent and reliable that it makes it easy for them to talk to you? Maybe in the past there have been times when you've got angry or upset and shown it. We only choose to talk to people if we feel they are approachable and we can rely on their reaction as well as their discretion. They spoil that just once and it's very difficult to get back. Trust can't just be created; we have to feel it inside and that takes an awful long time to build.

*...there aren't many people around who can see others as unique individuals with unique experiences.*

8

# Why some of us find it difficult to confide in others

There are a number of reasons why we choose not to confide in someone. For me, telling someone intimate details about how I feel and think does make me feel a little bit exposed and vulnerable. It's the fact that someone knows how I'm feeling, because then they may have expectations of how I should think and how I should behave. Another problem is that the issue I share is only a snapshot of how I feel in that given moment in time. Tomorrow, I may have moved on, but the snapshot and the associated judgements remain the same for the one I've told. Like a lot of people, I try and work it out for myself first which, unfortunately, can take quite a while. It's just that there aren't many people around who can see others as unique individuals with unique experiences.

One of the worse responses we can give someone is "oh yes, that happened to me, I know exactly what you're going through". They don't! We all react very differently to everything that happens to us. How our mind works involves our past as well as where we're going in the future. It's not just about the present moment because each experience we have incorporates what has happened in our life, which is different to anyone else's, and a future that contains personal hopes and dreams. The way that we, as individuals, interpret the world is so unique. For example, I expect you know of siblings who had practically the same upbringing and yet have very different perceptions of their childhood. They have such diverse attitudes, interpretations and relationships with their parents. This then ultimately shapes their own life and, of course, the relationships they have with others.

Family members, like parents, can often be the worse ones to confide in (unless you're really lucky). It's often because they care about you so much that it distorts their view of things and then they get into the habit of not showing the right sort of understanding. They want the best for you. But very often they can come across as being judgemental and end up telling you what you should be doing. It's so difficult for those really close not to be judgemental 'since to inform someone that he is good implies that you also have the right to tell him he is bad' (Rogers 1967, p55).

One problem is that people who help often see problems only from their own point of view and so how they would deal with something would be unique to them. Each of us can only interpret the world from inside our own head; we can never really see it from someone else's perspective. You may know friends and family that are very practical in their advice, but this can often be at the expense of a human connection, they don't see or truly understand you or how you feel. They may not even attempt to understand your point of view. For example, in some families there may be more concern about how outsiders perceive the family. It's not about you – it's about the honour of the family. This is why couples in some cultures often have to stay together, regardless. The problem here is that they end up living their life for someone else and by someone else's standards. Going against these values can be a massive dilemma, especially when they love their family.

*…we crave someone who really listens to us…*

# It's hard finding someone who will listen

If you don't have anyone close to you to confide in then it can be good talking to a complete stranger, like a counsellor, because there's no significant relationship involved that you have to worry about and no conditions. You're not friends and they'll more than likely let you do most of the talking – if they're any good. However, seeing a professional just seems to be a big step to take.

Another problem with confiding in others that are friends is that you can just end up listening to them and, if you do manage to get a word in, you can end up regretting it. The world is full of people who just want to talk at us. Walk down your road and count how many people talk at you as opposed to those who are interested in you. Those who are interested in you, and I don't mean nosey, are those who ask you questions and ask you how you feel about what is going on. A friend of mine was once talking to me in a locker room. He couldn't see because of the lockers between us. After about 5 or 10 minutes, I decided to go the toilet and when I came back he was still talking to me. A few minutes later, I went outside to put something in the car and when I came back he was still talking to me. You probably know people yourself like this where you don't actually need to be present for them to talk at you. They may ask you a question, but it's essentially put in as a link to what they want to tell you next. The irony is that they are the ones who think they know you really well and see themselves as one of your best friends. They base this on the fact that they are well-intentioned and if you were in trouble they would be there for you – not that you would want them there.

Alternatively, there are those out there who look at their

watch while you're talking to them. They try to do it sneakily, but we know what they're up to. Worst still are those who finish your sentences for you and then you have to wait to be allowed back into the conversation. Yet we crave someone who really listens to us and accepts us using the special type of listening that truly involves us. So few are good at active listening and yet, as the Ancient Greek philosopher Zeno observed, 'we have two ears and one mouth that we may listen the more and talk the less' (Laertius, 2013). So, what is it that you would talk about given the right person to confide in? In most cases it's about one of the most important elements in our lives – the relationship we have with our partner.

*You find yourself thinking about and caring more for a fictional character rather than your partner.*

## Your relationship

As I mentioned in the introductory chapter, there may be signs that indicate things are not as they used to be. You might be purposely going to bed at a different time to him just so that you can avoid that awkward moment when he may want to get amorous, or worst still, talk! You're beginning to wear nighties that cover your ankles and do up to the neck. Your underwear resembles the style your granny used to wear – the sort that you could put all your weekly shopping in. You find yourself thinking about and caring more for a fictional character rather than your partner. Little things are beginning to annoy you, the sort that you ignored in the early days – the way he clears his sinuses in the bathroom so loud that he can be heard in

12

Aberystwyth, while you're lying there with your ears plugged (I don't quite know why I chose Aberystwyth; it was just the first place I thought of), the way he examines his own ear wax or the fact that his nose hairs are now longer than the cat's whiskers. I don't know whether this is any consolation but it was probably his annoying little habits that prevented him from being with someone else.

You may just feel that the sparkle has gone out of your relationship and that you find yourself having totally different interests. Alternatively, he might want to do more things together. He's already dropped hints about buying a camping tent and threatened to take you with him. He wants to read you excerpts in bed from his *Owners' Manual* or *Steam Railway Illustrated*, but if you don't allow him to, what are you going to talk about? You might be always digging at each other, going through periods of not speaking or just arguing at any opportunity. You may be concerned about what life is going to be like when the kids leave home. If you recognise any of these signs don't worry, it's quite normal. But if you're not sure whether you really want to talk to someone about them then take a read of the following chapters – what have you got to lose?

In the next chapter, I concentrate on where you might be in your relationship and how getting to the stage where you can both talk is the only way forward, if that's what you want. I highlight some of the questions he dreads you asking because there's no right answer. If he's trying to please you and asks you what he can do for you there's something you should never say in response. I talk about marriage and suggest that those contemplating it need to be really clear just why they think theirs might work when so many others falter. The core of the chapter is about the difficulty of knowing how you feel, especially towards your partner. I explain that not wanting to be without someone is not the same as wanting to be with him or her. I finish with the concept of *love* and how this is different to being *in love* that is, very often, so short lived.

# Chapter Two

*Relationships and love*

In this chapter I cover:
- Getting to a stage when you can talk.
- Differences in communication and the questions he dreads.
- Being in a relationship and romance.
- How do you know how you feel?
- The meaning of love.
- Drifting apart – some of the signs.
- Taking a new direction.

> *…we know what hurts our partner and what areas are too sensitive. We know the places we just can't go.*

## Getting to a stage where you can talk

Analysing where you are in your relationship will obviously be your starting point for things to improve. For example, if you're in a position where you dread the kids not being around because it leaves both of you alone together, sooner or later you're going to have to confront the situation. It's not just going to go away and get better on its own, not without some sort of transplant for one of you. The essence of it all is that you've got to be in a position to talk adult-to-adult and this doesn't come easy. It's going to take time and patience, especially when one or both of you can't reach that adult level (I talk more about this in chapter four). If you do get the chance to talk don't have pre-set ideas of how he should respond, otherwise it's more like you're testing him and you'll end up disappointed. What I mean by this is don't read too much into it if he doesn't react the way you would want him to.

A friend of mine was having problems in her marriage to the point where she couldn't see any future together. He was out and about doing his own thing while she was studying and pursuing a career. They were never having time together at home without the kids. With little opportunity to talk, which became the norm over time, they had drifted apart. It got to the point where she felt he wouldn't engage. Finally, they set an evening aside to talk things through, but it didn't go well. At one point she suggested that she leave him. She was hoping that he would beg her to stay, but unfortunately there was no such response. She was horrified and upset by this as she had pre-determined what his reaction should be. However, in his mind, he thought that he'd already lost her through her going back to studying and developing her career. He felt it was what she wanted and didn't want to stand in her way. To him, it was just the confirmation he'd been expecting to hear. This is where fatal misunderstandings begin. There's no substitute for talking and telling your partner how you really feel – however hard it is.

Sometimes, couples keep their feelings to themselves about what hurts them and what they want in a partner because they don't want to force the other to do anything that they don't want to do. Couples have split up without realising that each other's needs were very similar. But then it's too late.

Tackling problems in a relationship can be difficult because it often means we are forced to confront issues in ourselves – possibly those that we've spent most of our adult life avoiding. In a relationship this avoidance can manifest itself where one partner is very controlling of the other. When someone assumes dominance it's difficult for those around them to question or confront them – sometimes we just need to choose the right battles. Consequently, the sensitive issues of the dominant partner are not acknowledged and therefore never dealt with. When we've been in a relationship for a long time, we know what hurts our partner and what areas are too sensitive – we know the places we just can't go. This is a problem with couples that fight a lot because getting angry during arguments is when the most hurtful comments are made, which are not easily retracted.

If you see yourself in this and want to work up to being able to talk then it's going to take time, it's not going to be achieved overnight. As you're the one gaining awareness of what's happening, I say this because it's you who is reading this book, you're the one who will probably have to take the first step. John Gray, the American relationship counsellor and author of the book *Men are from Mars, Women are from Venus*, recommends to start by avoiding criticism or advice unless it's asked for. If he receives a lecture he is likely to shut himself off and create distance. Instead work on giving him loving acceptance. Over time, as he begins to perceive this, he may start to notice a difference and then ask you what you think. 'Especially in an intimate relationship, men need to feel very secure before they open up and ask for support' (Gray 1993, p79).

> Instinctively men support one another by not offering advice or help unless specifically approached and asked. In coping with problems, a man knows he has to first go a certain distance by himself, and then if he needs help he can ask for it without losing his strength, power, and dignity. To offer help to a man at the wrong time could easily be taken as an insult.
>
> Gray 1993, p81

*These questions strike fear into a man because he knows it's already too late to retrieve the situation.*

## Communication

Men and women communicate in many different ways and this is often where misunderstandings begin.

Men mistakenly expect women to think, communicate, and react the way men do; women mistakenly expect men to feel, communicate, and respond the way women do. We have forgotten that men and women are supposed to be different. As a result our relationships are filled with unnecessary friction and conflict.

Gray 1993, p10

That's why men dread the classic question: 'which dress do you prefer me in?' His whole life flashes before him. The problem with this question is that he can't win. He'll feel he's giving you a compliment by saying how nice you look in one dress, but then he knows what's coming next: 'don't you like me in the other one?' It's a disaster! You don't understand the significance of this question, so unless he pleads insanity there's no way he can get out of it unscathed.

Other questions he dreads are: 'do you know what day it is?'
And worse still: 'have you noticed anything different?' These
questions strike fear into a man because he knows it's already
too late to retrieve the situation. However, there are worse
questions; questions which confirm his sexual inadequacy in
the bedroom:

- *Is it in yet?*
- *Are you done?*

There has to be tolerance on the part of both if the relationship
is going to survive without friction. Whereas women tend
to like to talk, men have a tendency to withdraw. You may
have noticed that he goes through phases when he mentally
disconnects from you for no apparent reason. It's just how men
act to think things through about the problems and issues they
face in their lives, at work and at home. If he does this, it's
usually better to wait for him to come back. If you hurry him
it could drive him even further away.

> If a man does not have the opportunity to pull away,
> he never gets a chance to feel his strong desire to be
> close. It is essential for women to understand that if
> they insist on continuous intimacy or "run after" their
> intimate male partner when he pulls away, then he will
> almost always be trying to escape and distance himself;
> he will never get a chance to feel his own passionate
> longing for love.
>
> Gray 1993, p94

Now, this is very important to note that, in the bedroom, if
your man asks you what you'd like him to do for you the last

thing you should say is 'I don't mind'. In instances like this he is seeking direction and he needs you to help him do the right things. He wants to please you. If you miss this opportunity then he continues to second-guess what you like, which means that he has to rely on his psychic powers once again. This is your opportunity so don't miss it, otherwise he might stop asking you.

*...the success of a relationship cannot be measured just by the fact that a couple stay together.*

## Being in a relationship

As a member of the human race we have an instinctual deep-seated belief in meeting someone special and living with them happily ever after. Unfortunately, evidence such as divorce statistics is stacked against us. We don't think when we get married that we'll add to these figures, but we invariably do. However, when it does happen and our relationship ends the human spirit tells us not to give up, so we have another go. Unfortunately, sixty to seventy per cent of second marriages fail and after that they increase even higher to seventy three/ seventy four per cent for third time lucky. Incidentally, I hope you're not reading this book over Christmas because January is the worse month apparently for divorces – it's when most people start off the process.

For some, marriage and divorce is more a way of life. Currently in the record books is a Mrs Linda Wolfe who has been married twenty three times, although this does include the three times she married the same man, as well as the one that only lasted three days. At her last wedding, she married her current husband Mr Glynn Wolfe. This was quite ironic as Mr Wolfe himself had already been married twenty eight times – now that's dedication.

There are, of course, those who avoid the divorce stats by making sure that when they marry, they don't marry another human being. There are isolated cases where people have married a dog, a dolphin, a snake, the Eiffel Tower and even the Berlin Wall (not the same person incidentally). There's even a case where a man during the marriage ceremony married himself – and not by mistake either. These tend to fall outside the parameters of our accepted normality.

Many relationships do survive, but the success of a relationship cannot be measured just by the fact that a couple stay together. How many people wake up in the morning after being married for over ten years and still say "Wow! I married the right person – I'm so lucky? How many couples do you know that are still together that you really admire? If I asked you to think of three couples whose relationship you would like to emulate, could you do it? Don't include TV celebrities because you don't really know them. Now think of five. My guess is that you are struggling to think of two. I used to know two very good marriages myself a few years ago; unfortunately, they are both divorced now. So if you are just starting out on your relationship, what makes you think your relationship will work when you see so many around you that don't, and so few that you want to use as a model for your own?

I know this all sounds rather pessimistic but I'm just trying to make you question yourself as to what you want and how you are going to achieve it. For example, would you or could you be with your partner if there was no physical attraction?

The reason I ask this is because if the answer is 'yes', then the relationship could have a good chance of working. If it's based on sex and that's the only thing you've got in common then I'm afraid it probably won't work. It's the same with beauty. If you choose someone because of his or her physical beauty then you're probably going to struggle in the future because there will always be more beautiful people around and you'll always be looking. Beauty and good sex is never enough.

There's no such person as 'Mr Right'. If you are looking for the perfect partner, even if he ticks all the right boxes, he still might not feel the same way about you as you do towards him. In most relationships, feelings are never exactly the same. One might feel stronger in some aspects but less in others. In most instances choosing someone is a compromise of some sort as everyone has imperfections. It's how your relationship develops which is of more importance. Therefore, you're better off looking for 'Mr Near-enough'. If you look for perfection to begin with, it's going to be all downhill from then on. You might be better off letting your love start slowly and allowing it to build up so that it has more of a foundation. What is intense and sparkles very early on can fizzle out once the *in love* stage passes.

Another factor that can draw our interest towards someone is the fact that they are attracted to us. We can find this very appealing, more-so than the person himself or herself. It's nice that someone likes us and finds us tempting and irresistible because it gives us a thrill – a feeling that we crave more of. But is it this alone that is carrying you along?

*Sex doesn't make up for a poor relationship.*

When relationships are young and people are attracted physically, more so than anything else, then the flaws in a relationship or the defects in a partner are often ignored. Think of the person you want to be with and imagine them old with their physical looks deteriorated. Would you still long to spend time with them? How do you know that how you feel today about someone will be just as strong or even stronger in five years time, ten years, thirty years? Are there big issues that you see now that you are ignoring or putting up with? Have you noticed his little ways? Either way you may not feel quite the same about them in the future as you do now.

Sex doesn't make up for a poor relationship. It might be okay for a short period, but not in the long term, even for men. Although the physical side is never far from their thoughts, being fantastic in bed isn't enough, or shouldn't be enough, for someone to stay. There has to be more because you can't just have sex all the time. You have to do other things in life and that means working as a partnership.

> I know, for example, that the best sex I have ever had was not important; the best sex I have ever had was with a girl called Rosie, whom I slept with just four times …She drove me mad, and I drove her mad and the fact that we had the knack of being able to come at the same time …counted for nothing.
>
> Hornby 2000, p58

## Romance

Being in love is lovely. The question in most films is: will the boy and girl get together by the end and live happily ever after? They better, that's why we've been watching. With the bombardment of all these romantic tales with happy endings, is it the thought of being in love that you like or are you actually in love? How do you know? Some make it fit because they want to experience the feeling of being in love. In a way they decide to fall in love and then choose the person to do it with. It's easy to be intoxicated with the thought of someone saying that they adore you. You may never have experienced that before and you like it. It might also be the idea of buying a home and filling it up with everything that is yours. When you're young you want all this stuff because it's a part of growing up and being an adult, and being seen as an adult with an adult identity. It's what everyone else seems to do.

For most of us this leads to marriage and getting married is a special occasion. I've known many young women who have talked to me endlessly about their wedding day. They talk about all the plans, the dress, who's been invited, the menu, where they're staying, what underwear they'll be wearing, but they never seem to tell me about their relationship (actually they don't really tell me about the underwear either; even when I ask). In fact, they've been a bit startled when I've asked why they are getting married. I suppose I ask them this because I want them to convince me that they've thought it through and not just focused on the wedding day (not that it's really any of my business). Rarely do they tell me about their feelings toward their future partner. It raises the question as to whether people choose this route because it's the accepted norm and because everyone else seems to do it, rather than an independent decision based on their relationship.

*...not wanting to be without someone is not the same as wanting to be with them.*

## How do you know how you feel toward your partner?

Sometimes it's so hard to know exactly how you feel. How do you know what you want? It could just be a reaction to something else. For example, if you have been in an abusive relationship but managed to come out of it, and then you meet someone who treats you really well, how do you know that you love that person? How do you know that you want to be with them all the time, or whether the comparison to your previous relationships is dominating your feelings? It can fool us when someone is in such stark contrast to what we've been used to. How can you be certain that it isn't just a sense of relief compared to what you've been through?

How do you know how you feel? It's something we tend not to assess until some emotional disaster strikes and forces the question. Sometimes when we've been with someone for a long time we lose track of how we feel towards him or her. Living with someone can be such a habit that we get used to it without thinking about it. When we do question ourselves we find that we don't know. It would be nice if someone could come down from above and tell us. However, there is another way. Neuro-linguistic writers Andreas and Faulkner (1996) discuss the motivation direction within us. We are either motivated towards something we want or away from something we don't want to happen. For example, think about the work that you do. Do you get something out of it and enjoy it, or is it a means to an end? If you didn't go you wouldn't earn enough money to live the life you want to. In other words, do you do something because you want to do it, or because if you didn't do it something negative could happen? In your relationship, are you together because you want to be with that person, or do you 'stay together out of loyalty and obligation or from the fear of starting over' (Gray 1993, p14)?

Sometimes you can be in a relationship and just not be sure whether you should stay with them or not. You can even linger in this indecisive state for many years without really being conscious of it. When you do think about it you're still not sure how you feel and what you want to do. If you know someone who is in this situation, ask them how they feel about their partner. If they say that they crave being with them, share the same values and like spending time with them then you'll be confident that they are motivated towards that person. But, as is often the case, they'll say 'I don't want to be on my own', I don't want to be left on the shelf', 'I might not meet anyone else', 'I couldn't afford the mortgage on my own', or even 'we have a child'. Their answers indicate that they are motivated away from something negative happening; something they don't want, or just don't want to face. It's the words they use that reveal how they feel about that person. That's why not wanting to be without someone is not the same as wanting to be with them.

This is obviously an important choice to make, but being the one who makes the decision to part is worse than having the decision thrust upon you, as you're the one who has to live with it. Therefore, you have to think things through thoroughly, that's not easy to say, let alone do. The last thing I want is for you to put down this book and go and dump your partner – especially if you haven't even finished the chapter yet. I don't want them blaming me for your actions; you have to think carefully and this takes time.

What do you want? That's the question you need to ask yourself. If you know that splitting up with someone would cause too much devastation within your family, or the guilt that you would have to live with would be unbearable then you've no decision to make – it's already made for you. This really depends on the type of person you are and only you know that.

Some try strategies to help save a relationship, something to disguise the fact that things are not right. The worse thing I've heard people say in situations like this is that they plan to have a baby because that would make everything all right. It doesn't, and it's not fair on the future child. In fact, having children usually is the start of the divide in relationships. Adding another member rarely helps. Ideally, relationships should have a solid foundation before anyone ever contemplates having children. I knew one couple that were desperate to have a child. They went through all sorts of treatments and during this time they were arguing and fighting, going through periods of separation and not talking. And yet it was a time when they should have been the most supportive to each other. This should have brought them closer. Instead it had the opposite effect. A baby would not have solved the problems in their relationship, but merely added to them.

Some couples seem to get into a habit of automatically arguing. When these start it's easy to drift off and forget what the argument is about. When people argue they tend to get angry and when they're angry they want to hurt. This ultimately ends up in them saying things that they regret and will dent each other's self-esteem. In fact, 'most couples start out arguing about one thing and, within five minutes, are arguing about the way they are arguing' (Gray 1993, p152).

*Some people are just simply better off living on their own.*

Arguments seem to start from nothing. I see couples in the supermarket and I can feel the tension between them when they're deciding on which brand of baked beans to buy. Some people are just simply better off living on their own. How on earth did they get together in the first place? There must have been a time when they went to bed together at the same time. They must have enjoyed each other's company at one time; they must have been in love at some point.

Being in love – now there's a topic!

## In love

A difficulty we have with the English language is that we tend to use the word 'love' to mean a variety of things: 'I love my cat', 'I love my children', 'I love you', and 'I love sausages'. It's all the same word, but people rarely marry their favourite sausage, so what's the difference between 'love' and being 'in-love'? For this section, I refer to *The Road Less Travelled*, the work of American psychiatrist Morgan Scott Peck (1990); as well as the contributions of psychotherapist Robin Skynner and comedian John Cleese (1993b) from their book *Life and How to Survive it*. I do this because the authors give a different take on the traditional concept of love and being in love, and how sex plays its part.

> …the experience of falling in love is specifically a sex-linked erotic experience. We do not fall in love with our children even though we may love them very deeply. We do not fall in love with our friends of the same sex – unless we are homosexually orientated – even though we may care for them greatly. We fall in love only when we are consciously or unconsciously sexually motivated.
>
> Scott Peck 1990, p72

This is why, maybe, when we are in-love we feel so alive and everything in the world seems so much brighter. Some are desperate to feel this way and can fool themselves into believing they are in-love, because they want to have that feeling. That is why the choice of person is sometimes immaterial and often inappropriate – they make it fit.

> We are as likely to fall in love with someone with whom we are obviously ill matched as with someone more suitable. Indeed, we may not even like or admire the object of our passion, yet, try as we might, we may not be able to fall in love with a person whom we deeply respect and with whom a deep relationship would be in all ways desirable.
>
> Scott Peck 1990, p77

*The myth of love…in a way ensures the survival of the species.*

I expect you know couples that are in love. There's no getting through to them. They can be on another planet and all common sense seems to desert then. Fortunately, or unfortunately, it is often only a relatively brief period of time that they stay in this state.

> …the experience of falling in love is invariably temporary. No matter whom we fall in love with, we sooner or later fall out of love if the relationship continues long enough. This is not to say that we invariably cease loving the person with whom we fell in love. But it is to say that the feeling of ecstatic lovingness that characterised the experience of falling

in love always passes. The honeymoon always ends.
The bloom of romance always fades.

Scott Peck 1990, pp72-73

When couples do come out of the 'in love' phase, they are inevitably married and on their way to having children. The myth of love, as Scott Peck calls it, in a way, ensures the survival of the species that we should be grateful for. If our parents didn't go through that temporary period of being in love, most of us wouldn't be around today. Without sex, they wouldn't have got together in the first place, they would have stayed as friends. Therefore, sex is the reason why we're all here – but I expect you knew that.

The thing is, people cling on to the myth and it creates the illusion that it will last forever. It doesn't, but 'people waste vast amounts of energy desperately and futilely attempting to make the reality of their lives conform to the unreality of the myth' (Scott Peck 1990, p80).

If you believe that meeting the right person is written in the stars or that fate has played its hand then I'm afraid it's the same logic as saying 'white rabbits' at the beginning of each month with an 'R' in it. It indicates there's someone up there in charge of people saying 'white rabbits' at precisely the right moment as there is someone else in charge of relationships and that's all he or she is responsible for. As we have the highest divorce rate in history, and as most of us can't think of more than two couples whose relationship we admire, they're not doing a particularly good job. Either their filing system is all to pot or they are desperately in need of an assistant.

Being in this 'in love' phase has elements of dependency about it and a lot of marriages are a product of this, not of love itself. I've heard of some couples being so in love they help brush each other's teeth, that might be the first thing to go; in fact, I'd put money on it that they won't be doing that this time next year if they're living together. They may also find that just one of them will be wearing their onesie at half past six in the evening. Behaviour towards each other changes over time, even the activity of talking. Apparently new lovers spend seventy five per cent of their time gazing into each other's eyes when they talk rather than the thirty to sixty per cent average of other couples. But we love this phase because it makes us feel alive even though it automatically brings with it insecurity. When we feel we have something precious there is always a fear of losing it.

# Dependency

Love can mean the enjoyment of intimacy but through togetherness and separateness. In opposition to this is dependency. One is classed as healthy; the other unhealthy. With the unhealthy love, it involves someone being reliant on someone else for happiness. In situations like this being together is essential. There's anxiety about being apart and the thought of not being able to live without them.

But what about the great love stories of all time? – Romeo and Juliet, La Traviata, Carmen, Antony and Cleopatra? As Skynner and Cleese (1993b, pp13-14) put it:

> 'Oh, they're so wonderful aren't they, so romantic.'
> 'Well, they're not wonderful. They are tales of almost unmitigated misery. There's not ten minutes of good, everyday happiness and fun in any of them. The lovers usually get one dollop of over-the-top ecstasy and apart from that it's wall-to-wall suffering. They get stabbed, walled up in tombs, they throw themselves under trains, or commit suicide with asps, they poison themselves and die of consumption or renounce each other in agony. They're convinced they can only find happiness with one other person, whom they deliberately choose on grounds of unavailability. So …why do you think all this dependence and its consequent suffering is equated with true love?

Scott Peck (1990) calls it 'passive dependent behaviour' where individuals look to others as the main source of happiness and fulfilment. In the end, if they are not happy they have someone to blame. He takes this further by saying:

In summary, dependency may appear to be love because it is a force that causes people to fiercely attach themselves to one another. But in actuality it is not love; it is a form of antilove.

Scott Peck 1990, p93

*Unfortunately, if you always rely on another human being for your happiness there's a very good chance that you will always be disappointed.*

When someone is dependent on their partner for their own happiness care is mainly centred, not on the other but on themselves. Unfortunately, if you always rely on another human being for your happiness, there's a very good chance that you will always be disappointed. This is possibly why Shakespeare claimed Romeo and Juliet as a tragedy, not a love story. It was a love that relied on emotion in the present moment and their choice of partner was always going to be doomed from the start, that's why they chose them. This unhealthy love is something the music industry, for example, has relied so heavily upon. Take a few song titles and lyrics at random:

- '4 seasons of loneliness' – Boys2Men
- 'I should be lost without you' – David Condos
- 'I'm a slave for 4 u' – Britney Spears
- 'I can't breathe unless I'm with you' – Clingy
- 'If you leave me I shall swop names on a hospital bed of someone who's going to have a heart transplant' – Anguish & Misery

Actually, the last couple I made up, but you get the idea.

35

When you require another individual for your survival, you are a parasite on that individual. There is no choice, no freedom involved in your relationship. It is a matter of necessity rather than love. Love is the free exercise of choice.

Scott Peck 1990, p86

When someone is reliant on his or her partner jealously is never far away. This originates from a need to control the other in the relationship, which often stems from a lack of confidence or self-esteem. 'If one half has no clear idea of who they are, or has low self-esteem, it can seem more comfortable to them to hide in a couple than to re-establish a separate, parallel identity' (Marshall 2007, p36).

## Healthy love – separately together

For a healthy love to exist, there is closeness and distance at the same time where both are capable of great intimacy and affection, but it is balanced out by both being self-sufficient at the same time. Healthy love is a combination of separateness and togetherness.

> …the genuine lover always respects and even encourages this separateness and the unique individuality of the beloved. Failure to perceive and respect this separateness is extremely common, however, and the cause of much mental illness and unnecessary suffering.
>
> Scott Peck 1990, p149

It's not a case where you live, or have, totally separate lives and interests; it's not a loveless relationship, so don't think that you've achieved this healthy love just because you don't want to see each other. It's where you are independent and you respect the independency of your partner. You still crave being with that person and look forward to seeing them. You can't wait until you're both just on your own and sharing time together. You miss them when you're apart and that's a nice feeling to have because it can help you appreciate the togetherness more. That's why not living together all the time can work as long as there's commitment in the relationship. However …

Deep commitment does not guarantee the success of the relationship but does help more than any other factor to assure it. Initially shallow commitments may grow deep with time; if not, the relationship will likely crumble or else be inevitably sickly or chronically frail.

Scott Peck 1990, p128


## Drifting apart

Hectic lives can come between a relationship where all of a sudden, although you speak, you don't get the time to talk anymore. This is often the case when children come along. The intimacy is sacrificed between you through 'the hustle and bustle of life or the pressure of bringing up children' (Marshall 2007, p115).

When the patter of tiny feet come along so much of our energy has to be directed on to them (no, not just the feet, I meant the whole thing), which means that partners are too knackered when they come together. As time goes on, the distance can grow and often without noticing it. It then evolves into a habit and then a way of life. The sensual fire that you once had has burnt low and you've got into a routine. After a while, you find that you've not said 'I love you' for quite some time with any meaning, and suddenly to utter those words now makes you feel awkward, so you don't. You're not even in a position to talk it through, often because you don't really know what to say or how to say it. You stop doing things you used to do like holding hands when you're out. That's why when you have children you need to make sure that there are opportunities for just the two of you to be together, even a weekend away now and again.

Nothing prepares you for having children. You go from not having any to having them, it's like one extreme to the other. It's not like you can go on a training course and get a diploma in parenthood. When they're ill or playing up you're relying on your own up-bringing experience and it's then you realise you're saying things that your parents used to say to you. So much is involved with their childhood that it seems much more than a full time job, draining your energy. Your own relationship has to fit in and you can find yourselves just going through the motions, not having the time or the strength to sort out issues that you know need sorting.

*Ultimately, you can end up distracting yourself from what's really happening.*

## Is there something wrong?

You may be in a position where deep down you know something is wrong. What happens is that it gets disguised. The signs that indicate something is lacking in the relationship are often not realised at the time. For example, it might be that you're always going away on holiday with other couples. Maybe you don't even think of going away by yourselves. You spend less time together and have not thought about whether it's enough. One of you may have become more involved with a hobby as a substitute. Sports like golf or fishing can take over because it takes one of you away from the family home for hours on end. You might be spending more time planning your next tattoo rather than what you want to do with your partner. It could be that you're collecting more and more pets to fill up your home so your partner gets lost in the crowd. People are always popping round so you've always got a house-full. Do you always like to have people around you so that you're never on your own? Is the TV constantly on, even in the bedroom?

These may or may not be signs that something is wrong, but you may feel real issues are easier to ignore than talk about because of the hassle involved. Ultimately, you can end up distracting yourself from what's really happening. The reality might be that you might not be happy or you feel you are not progressing as an adult. 'Pastimes and games are substitutes for the real living of real intimacy' (Berne 1964, p18).

In any love relationship, whether we acknowledge it or not, we change as people. We move on as life evolves around us. This creates changes in relationships and 'problems arise because people assume their partner will always have the same needs as at the start of the relationship, but life changes us and our expectations' (Marshall 2007, p42). That's why a significant point in a lot of relationships is when the children leave home. For so long they have been at the centre of everything you've done and now suddenly it's just the two of you again. This takes a lot of readjusting, especially when you don't believe you have anything in common anymore. This is a time when a lot of relationships seem to break up, because the real issues can no longer be hidden or disguised.

## Taking a new direction

The children are more self-sufficient or have left home and now you may be thinking of what to do with your life. In today's society, there seems to be more and more pressure to get higher qualifications just to stand a chance of initiating that career you're interested in. For a lot of women, education offers a new direction. However, it is well documented that women often don't get the support from their partners in the same way that men do. It has also been suggested that returning to education, particularly higher education, is the first step that causes a rift in relationships. In reality, cracks were already there. It's the fact that when someone goes back to education it highlights that one is progressing and mentally maturing when the other is not. Seeing this can fuel his insecurity, which accentuates the difficulties in the relationship. It's just that a lot of men do like to have some control over their partner and when the woman is making decisions and moving on it creates an imbalance in power for men in the home. This is why it can be hard for women because of the expectations others have of them. They have to carry on and do all the duties in the home they were doing before just to show that going back to education won't upset the household. However, there comes a point where they either carry on as if nothing is wrong or confront it. Either way, the consequence is a lack of love and affection, which can make them feel more and more isolated.

If we feel our needs are not being met with our partner, it is tempting to let someone else satisfy them. This is how affairs begin. The reasons why people have affairs, and the types of affair they have, is something I look at in the next chapter. Find out the real truth about 'no-strings attached' relationships, the one-day of the year you're more likely to get caught, and the nice feelings we get when opportunities do come our way.

# Chapter Three

## *Affairs*

In this chapter I cover:
- Why people have affairs.
- The feelings associated with having an affair.
- Is one of you totally to blame?
- How the fantasy of an affair compares in reality.
- Getting caught and the worst excuse.
- The types of affairs people have.

*As we get older we still have the same temptations, it's just
that we don't get the same opportunities.*

## Why people have affairs

Affairs have always happened and will always happen. Most
don't purposely go out looking to have an affair, they just seem
to drift into one. It can easily happen when you've been in a
relationship for a long time and then suddenly someone else
starts showing you some attention and finding you attractive.
It could have been years since you've experienced that enjoyable
feeling of someone flirting with you and being interested in
you. It's nice to feel desired once again, that we haven't lost
the old magic. It's quite normal to feel like this. Also, there's

a fear that comes along as we get older, that this might be the last time we get to feel like this. If you believe that you are not particularly attractive to the opposite sex it can be worse, because you may see it as the only opportunity of making love to someone else before you snuff it. When people are old nearing the end of their life and reflecting on their regrets they don't generally say: 'I wish I'd watched more TV', or 'I wish I'd spent more time at work'. No, it's more likely they think 'I wish I'd had more sex with more people' or 'I wish I'd been single longer'. So, when opportunities come our way we feel that we should take them while we can. As we get older, we still have the same temptations, it's just that we don't get the same opportunities.

For those of you who are attractive and attracted to the opposite sex on a continual basis, there will always be temptation. If that's your weakness then it will be a constant struggle for you throughout your whole life, whomever you have chosen to be with. We all have our personal weaknesses whether they be money, power, drink, drugs, recognition, sex, or chocolate hob-nobs – things that we desire, but we know will bring trouble. These stay with us for most of our lives as 'whatever you resist, persists' (O'Connor and Seymour 1993, p11).

## The feeling associated with having an affair

We can easily forget the passion and the intensity associated with courting and it's just so arousing to feel it again. We often lose that thrill we get in our stomach of just thinking about being with someone – another reason not to live together. We all crave affection and love and if that is lacking in our lives then we're drawn to someone offering it to us, even though we may not even like the person. Flirting is exciting, but deep down we know that we are flirting with danger. It may be a fantasy of ours to touch someone new, to feel their body touching ours and to feel intimate with someone like they do in the films. There may also be more to it than just physical desire. Giving his thoughts on the matter Abraham Maslow (1970, p9) says 'an individual going through the whole process of sexual desire, courting behaviour, and consummatory love making may actually be seeking self-esteem rather than sexual gratification'.

I'm sure many more would have an affair if they didn't calculate just how much they could lose if they got caught and it meant the end of their marriage. For others, it's almost a way of life. They not only cheat on their wife but also on their girlfriend. The most notable example of this is found in the following account:

> Fredrick Augustus was Elector of Saxony and later King of Poland. When he died in 1699, his household records revealed that he had produced only one child in wedlock. It was called Maurice. However the records also showed that Augustus' marital devotion occasionally faltered. He was also responsible for 345 illegitimate children.
>
> Pile 1980, p196

Regrettably, having an affair does come with a price. There's no such thing as a 'no-strings attached' relationship. One will always want more from it than the other, particularly as time goes by and the longer the relationship continues. Feelings are not always easy to predict and they don't stay the same. For example, you can't both possibly guarantee that your feelings won't have evolved in three years' time. Ideally when you set out on an affair it would be ideal to get the other person to sign a contract stipulating what is and isn't involved and scheduling a get-out clause for you at any point. Unfortunately, before you go and get a sheet of paper and a pen, this is a very cold and clinical thing to do. Generally, this is not in the minds of those starting out anyway. When people think of having an affair they think very much about the present moment and not about the future, not even about next week.

Even if your feelings don't change you will still have to deal with the deceit. Having an affair means that you will have to lie and, if you do lie, then you need a very good memory to recall what it is you've lied about. The longer it goes on the more chance you'll be found out and there will be stressful times when everyone wants a bit of you on the same day. Apparently, the one-day that most people are caught by their partner is Valentine's Day. The reason for this is that there are more texts received on that day as there is more correspondence expected. And since the introduction and common use of the mobile phone many have been caught out sending a text to the wrong person.

Then, there's the guilt. When sex was invented it was added as a main ingredient. However, some don't feel it; they think that by keeping their socks on in bed means that they haven't been completely unfaithful; some minds work this way. There are others who feel the guilt but don't allow themselves to think about it, whilst for others it destroys their life. They are always analysing the pros and cons and when the disadvantages begin to outweigh the advantages then they have to end it. It's a recipe of deceit, lies and worry. Then, to cleanse themselves they own up, which is a very selfish act in itself. They do it to make themselves feel better and in a way send out an invitation to be punished. In fact, the whole idea of confession is based on this idea. Once they've confessed then, hopefully, they can carry on as if nothing has happened. Unfortunately, they leave in their path hurt, pain and a mistrust, which may never be healed. So many couples who have gone through this try to make a go of their relationship again only to find that things have changed too much. Invariably, they end up parting further down the line.

*If they are not getting those needs satisfied with you, then it increases the temptation when someone else offers it.*

## Is one of you totally to blame?

If you do find out that your partner has had an affair it is going to be painful, but after you've been through the hurt and anger you need to reflect on whether you've contributed yourself towards it in some way. An affair is very often a symptom of a problem rather than the actual problem itself. Unfortunately, others are very quick to judge.

> After an affair society certainly likes to label the 'guilty' party, who cheated, and the 'innocent' party, who was cheated on. Yet in my experience the circumstances are always much murkier.
>
> Marshall 2007, p58

We all have needs, we're all human and, as I've said previously, being human can be really difficult at times.

Have you stopped showing affection, have you mentally disconnected, do you show your partner the love that he or she needs? This can be why partners look elsewhere or just notice the interest others show in them. The need to love and to be loved is part of our make-up as mentioned at the beginning of the book. It's part of being human and if we don't find it in one place then we go somewhere else in search of it, unless it finds us first. So don't stop trying just because you're married, you've still got to work at your relationship. We all need to feel love on a continual basis and it has a positive effect on us when we do. 'Men are motivated and empowered when they feel needed …women are motivated and empowered when they feel cherished' (Gray 1993, p43). If they are not getting those needs satisfied with you, then it increases the temptation when someone else offers it. There is always an increased appreciation and desire for things the more they are in short supply.

## How the fantasy of an affair compares in reality

Very often, when people have affairs, they begin to realise that the problems they have in their own marriage reoccur. The reason for this is that wherever we go we take our baggage with us. The attractive thing about an affair is that it doesn't usually come with all the everyday mundane stuff you have to do when you live with someone. For a start there are no household chores. There's no going to the supermarket for the weekly shopping, no kids to taxi around, no housework and no emptying the bins. There are not even any annoying little habits to worry about that seem to surface later. In a way, it's a fantasy.

Skynner and Cleese (1993b) explain that the desire to have an affair can put a lot of strain on a relationship. This is especially the case when couples have been together since they were childhood sweethearts and have not had much experience with other partners. As they may have missed out on stages of their adolescence, there is a tendency to glamorise relationships with others. They get to the point when they compare their partner to a perfect fantasy and cling on to it. This is derived from romantic novels and no relationship can ever reach these standards. The fantasy can ruin a relationship. This can be one of the drawbacks of couples marrying too young. There's a feeling at some point that they've missed out and they want to recapture it before it's too late. When we're young, we're so sure of how we feel and that the feelings we have will last forever. In reality, they very rarely do.

If you married young and to someone much older than yourself, it's not until a few years later that you begin to feel the real difference in your ages. It didn't seem to matter years ago and although people said to you at the time that the age difference was too much you just didn't believe them. It didn't matter to you then, but it does now. The biggest age difference I'm aware of is where a twenty two year-old woman married a man who was 105. If she doesn't feel the age difference now she surely will in her forties.

50

## Getting caught and the worst excuse

Another problem of having an affair is being caught. Very often the guilty partner feels very sorry for the hurt and the pain they've caused, but it's debatable whether it's because they got caught or whether they actually did feel that way. If they did feel that way, then they would've felt bad whether they got caught, or not. And, if they did feel guilty, then they might have ended it earlier – it's something like that anyway.

The problem with having an affair is that there is always a chance of being caught or having to explain something quite unusual as is shown in the following example.

In 1976 Dr Brian Richards of Deal in Kent discovered one of the great love stories of all time, while in Regent's Park, London. He came across a semi-clad gentleman who had slipped a disc while enjoying himself in the back of a sports car with his girl-friend. Since the man was transfixed with agony, his girl-friend was unable to get out for help. In desperation she jammed her foot against the hooter button. This attracted Dr Richards, an ambulanceman, a fireman and a large crowd of passers-by who formed a circle around the car. 'You'll never get them out of there,' said the fireman who then set about cutting the back off the car.

Trained for desperate situations, two women voluntary workers arrived and began serving hot sweet tea through the window. 'It was like the blitz,' one of them commented.

Eventually, the lover was carried off in agony. Ambulancemen told the girl-friend that his recovery prospects were good. 'Sod him,' she replied. What's worrying me is how I shall explain to my husband what's happened to his car'.

Pile 1980, p193

What this story highlights is how absurd and ridiculous the action of sex really is when you come to think of it. You get into all sorts of strange positions to try to bring together bodily parts for docking, which, at times, seem ill-suited for the purpose. It can feel like being on a wildlife programme, especially when the cat seems to be watching.

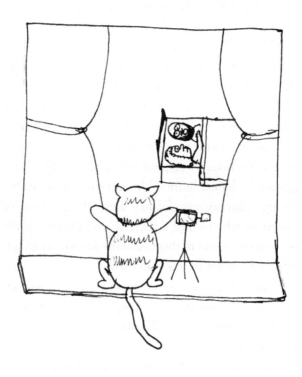

Affairs start slowly under the heading of 'just friends'. This belief that there's no harm in it is really just to convince themselves. However, if it is just based on friendship, then there would be less need for it all to be done in secret as 'true friendship is open to public scrutiny; inappropriate friendship is concealed' (Marshall 2007, 148).

Getting caught obviously leads to excuses and there are none finer than the following example:

During his divorce hearing in July 1978, a London window cleaner was asked to explain what he and 'the other woman' were doing in his bedroom with the lights out. He replied: 'Playing snooker.' The judge ... said: 'To my mind it is rather difficult to play a game of snooker in a room where the lights are off.'

Mr Charlton was next asked to explain the noises of passionate abandon which his wife heard coming from the house. He replied that it was 'an expression of surprise or disappointment made when playing a difficult shot.'

He was then asked why, on another occasion, the 'other woman' had been seen undressed from the waist down. Mr Charlton's explanation was that she 'was doing some sewing and altering her slacks.'

His wife did not believe it and nor did the judge.

Pile 1980, pp199-200

*The workplace still remains the number one environment for adultery.*

## The types of affairs people have

For this final section I refer to the work of author and editor David Moxon (2001, p49) as he sums it all up very neatly in his book about relationships. He explains the reasons why people have affairs.

> Access to other people – modern Western society has provided men and women with vast opportunities to meet new people on a daily basis. The workplace still remains the number one environment for adultery.

Moxon continues by referring to Eaker *et al.* (1993) who state that for women entering into an affair, it is essentially a cry for help when their current partner is no good. They go on to identify five types of affairs:

### The avoidance-distancing affair.

This is where the adulterer uses an affair to distance himself or herself, or even avoid a relationship that he or she is finding lacking in intimacy. This is particularly common with men.

### The peacemaking affair.

This is an affair whose aim is to assess what is lacking or wrong with a person's 'main relationship'. The adulterer is ironically using it as a desperate attempt to 'rescue' his or her failing existing relationship. Often this type of affair is nothing more than a one-night stand.

### The escape hatch.

Many find it difficult to end a relationship, even if they are very unhappy. Often this type of affair gives people a reason to leave. Women tend to engage in this type more than men.

### Love-seeking.

Many affairs are based upon flattery ...all humans possess a fundamental need to be liked and needed. Often affairs take place when individuals are reaching a crucial milestone in their lives. End-of-decade birthdays are very common times, when people start to feel insecure about their age and their need to feel wanted.

### Compulsion.

This is adultery driven by hedonistic urges. Adulterers who fall into this category have little regard for the feelings of others and often engage in affairs for purely sexual reasons.

(Moxon 2001, p49)

Affairs can happen because we feel that we're not with the right person, or that we just don't seem to connect with them anymore. It might simply be that we are different now, we've moved on mentally. In a way we may feel that we've outgrown our partner. Yet in the beginning everything seemed to be fine.

For a lot of us the partner we have was our own choice, but when the relationship changes over time and perhaps things turn sour we can question ourselves as to how we could have got it so wrong. I tell you how you probably got it wrong in the next chapter and why this is quite a normal thing to do. I look at what it is that influences us in choosing our partner, not just the physical attributes we like, but the factors that we are unaware of. Here, I introduce you to your 'screen' and what's behind it. I look at why we behave or react in certain ways as an adult and where these behaviours stem from. I conclude by identifying what needs to be in place if a couple are to communicate effectively and why, when things are not right, there can be hidden meaning in the conversations they have.

# Chapter Four

*Choosing a partner and how communication breaks down*

In this chapter I cover:
- What we physically look for in a partner.
- Learning stages of development in our upbringing.
- Our partner – the unconscious choice.
- Why we are so like our parents.
- Understanding communication.

'Each person's family script will influence not only their personality but their choice of partner' (Marshall 2007, p157). This may seem a very strange quote to start off with, especially when the thoughts of our families may be furthest from our minds when we choose someone to fall in love with. So how do we choose a partner and what is it that determines who we choose? In reality, when we first meet someone the initial attraction we have is really based on very limited information. As there is so much going on that we are unaware of I'll be approaching the topic from a slightly unusual angle. I'm going to recount the work of Skynner and Cleese (1993a, 1993b) in this chapter, because their deductions about attraction help us to make sense of our own behaviour which, ultimately, determines how we communicate with our partner.

## What we physically look for in a partner

In finding someone attractive we're all aware of what we physically prefer. We know what we like. I know men who go for blonds, or they look for a certain sophistication, short skirts, long straight hair, short curly hair, black fingernails, high heels, brown eyes or a big chest. I even know some men who look for intelligence – but not many. As for women, they may go for someone smart, short hair, bald, tall, short, with nice teeth or clean fingernails. There are some who like to inspect a man's shoes first – the list goes on. It might be a particular culture or the skin colour we prefer. We know what we like and we can't help it. Therefore, we all have conscious likes and dislikes.

However, if the majority of us have chosen our partner ourselves why is it that we have such a high divorce rate? Even those who are still together may also be wondering why not many of us are good at choosing the right partner. The reason for this is because the choice is often made at an unconscious level. To explain this I need to go back in time.

*...we find ourselves acting in many ways like our parents did.*

## Stages of development in our upbringing

As we were growing up, we had to go through stages of development. These were stages where we had to learn how to behave in order to prepare us for adulthood. It included all sorts of things like dealing with anger, being the centre of attention, discipline, friendships, independence, authority, praise, sadness, love, affection, dealing with the opposite sex, honesty, apologising, affection – it's a long list. Essentially, they are all about handling emotions, feelings and behaviours. For many of these, we relied on our family to guide us through. Unfortunately, as you may already know, not all were tackled. When you think about your own family, you'll recognise that some of these stages were open and some were closed. The open ones were those that were spoken about and dealt with, so the likelihood is that you learnt that stage. However, there were those that were guarded or hidden and therefore never discussed. Therefore, the stage was never learnt.

Think about the people you know. You can possibly sense which stages of development they've had problems with. You probably know someone who just can never apologise, even when all the evidence is stacked against them. You surely know those who find it difficult to show love or affection, or who can't give any sort of praise. Often those who can't give praise find it difficult to accept praise. You definitely know someone who's not learnt how to deal with anger, you may even be living with them. You may have entered the relationship believing that you could change them, but it very, very, rarely works out that way.

The reason why some of these emotions were closed and not dealt with in families was because our parents also had problems with the same stages when they were growing up with their family. It's passed down from generation to generation and so because they didn't learn how to handle a particular stage we can't learn it from them.

Fortunately, if we miss a stage in our childhood we can learn it later on. We can learn things like love and affection vicariously through others and we can emulate the qualities of those around us whom we admire. The problem is that if we don't learn it later on we know deep down that we have difficulty dealing with that emotion and it can make us feel uncomfortable. We respond by pretending that we haven't missed that particular stage by over compensating in our behaviour. In other words, we try to control the way others perceive us. For example, take learning and talking about sex. It's difficult to get the hang of when we're young so most of us are more comfortable about dealing with this topic when we grow up, after we've had a bit of practice. But if someone hasn't learnt this stage then they can feel embarrassed about talking about sex and so they try to hide it. They do this by pretending that they're okay with the subject and therefore influencing the way they are perceived. With men, in particular, they can do this by telling really crude jokes or sniggering at any mention of anything to do with sex. When you don't laugh with them they can accuse you of having a problem with sex, but all along they're deflecting the issue away from themselves on to you.

Our families have a huge influence on our upbringing and the way we deal with life as an adult. It's to do with learning and there are a lot of theories about it. Essentially, most of it is unconscious as it's about copying and modelling others' behaviour. This is why we find ourselves acting in many ways like our parents did. At the other extreme, in society, it explains why the abused sometimes become the abusers.

Missing a stage can feel like a weakness, but by acting long enough as though the stage has not been missed we can believe our own pretences over time. Our behaviour becomes such a habit that we end up 'hiding the fact that we've failed to grow up in some way …we end up hiding it *from ourselves*' (Skynner and Cleese 1993a, p28). If a stage is not learnt it stays with us and then it continues to get passed on to our children.

'They fuck you up, your mum and dad' said the English poet Phillip Larkin in High Windows (1999, p24). He recognised that they didn't mean to, but accepts that they were also 'fucked up' by their parents. Although he didn't really acknowledge that parents pass on good things as well as the bad he did conclude that the only way to stop it happening was by not having children to pass the faults on to.

This, of course, means that we take our families with us wherever we go and they are always there in whatever we do – it's what we do as humans and it goes on unconsciously. Emotions and behaviours that are not dealt with become locked behind a screen. 'The bad ones get put behind the screen and the entire family has a kind of unspoken but very powerful agreement that the feelings behind the screen mustn't be noticed' (Skynner and Cleese 1993a, p31).

The problem is that the screen slips up and down now and again and if there is a lot behind the screen it can take masses of energy keeping it in place. Therefore, when things do come out they can be uncontrollable. For example, you may have been in the company of someone who has anger or jealously issues behind their screen and what it can be like when it does escape – it can be quite destructive.

> As a rule of thumb, the fewer the emotions hidden behind the screen the more emotionally healthy the individual. Some people have low screens and find it easier to look behind at the difficult emotions; others have such high and thick screens that they are totally unaware of their off-limits subjects.
>
> Marshall 2007, p59

The question now is: how does this relate to choosing a partner?

*It's only when issues are at the forefront of consciousness that they can be dealt with effectively.*

## Our partners – the unconscious choice

People are attracted to those with similar backgrounds. They choose those who seem to have missed out on the same developmental stage, so it invariably turns out that both had problems with the same feeling or the same behaviour.

Obviously, you don't know what's behind someone's screen

when you first meet them. You might get glimpses when you go out with them or if you go away for a weekend, but generally you don't really know until you start to live with them (although mothers seem to know somehow – radar perhaps). What attracts you to someone is not what is behind the screen but what you are allowed to see in front, the shop window as it were, because what you see in his shop window is similar to what you have in your shop window showcased to disguise and hide what's behind your screen. In other words, what you are allowed to see in someone else has similarities with what you allow others to see in you. Therefore, you make connections and can see similarities. And what attracts people is having things in common even though they may not realise what they are.

There can also be fascination about what is behind someone's screen when couples first meet. However, when they are in love with each other, they turn a blind eye to the possible faults because they want it to work so much – hence, they make it fit. They don't allow their minds to dwell on them. However, sooner or later these faults get noticed more.

Relationships that work are those where each person is tolerant of what is behind their partner's screen and acknowledge and confront what is behind their own. They are prepared to look behind their own screens and go through temporary discomfort, deal with it, accept it, and move on. Although admitting to weaknesses is difficult to handle and makes people feel vulnerable, the more they can admit to the better. It's only when issues are at the forefront of consciousness that they can be dealt with effectively.

With other relationships, there can be a lot behind the screens. There can be a refusal to talk about things and defiance against admitting to anything. You perhaps know not to raise certain subjects with those close to you. To raise the screen would not be worth it as it can be too painful and people end up defending themselves. They can react angrily at the slightest bit of criticism, which as you may know is only painful if there's some truth in it. In circumstances like these self-image becomes dented. In many relationships, it is here where the female often protects the male ego. She knows not to confront certain issues, so he carries on believing there's nothing wrong. However, there are some women, the astute and clever ones, who have the ability to use this to their own advantage by acting as if their man is always getting his own way, when in reality he's not – she is.

You may know of one or two quite destructive relationships where the couple are always bickering with each other. They can be quite cutting and patronising to one another and can slip in and out of this at any time. What attracted them to each other in the first place? It could have been a witty and sarcastic conversation that appealed. It might have been the fight against authority or the showing of individuality that they could connect with. Now the bickering couple rely on each other. They need each other. If they keep blaming the other for the situation, it prevents each of them from having to examine themselves. In circumstances like this, they need each other because if they keep fighting the devil in their partner they can conclude – 'I am like I am because of you', 'I'm always having to deal with you'. Eric Berne, the founder of transactional analysis (1964), calls this the *If it weren't for you* game. There's always an excuse for who they are and how they are as long as they are with their partner. 'When things go pear shaped it is easier to believe that there is something wrong with our other half because, if they are not the problem, we are' (Godson 2011, p165). If they were then to separate at some point they would have to come to terms with themselves. Fortunately for us, when we see really destructive relationships like this, we can feel rest assured that they are 'married to each other and not making two other people miserable' (Skynner and Cleese 1993a, p48).

I must point out, as do Skynner and Cleese, that if you recognise yourself in this then it can't all be locked behind your screen, otherwise you wouldn't recognise it. Those who have lots behind their screen have not acknowledged it for so long it's become habit. They've become so used to their own behaviour that they wouldn't recognise it (if that makes sense). The problem is how to deal with it if this does apply to you because it's about handling unlearnt stages of development, and for most people it's about growing up. From this, we can see that our behaviour stems from the way we internalised our upbringing and why we chose our partner, but how does it influence us with regards to our ability to communicate in our relationships?

*That's his fault ... I'll kill him when I get home!'*

# Adulthood – we're so similar to our parents

> Have you ever found yourself reacting to something just as one of your parents would – perhaps in a way you've vowed you never would – and then wondered how much of your personality is inherited? To what degree are you really like your mother or your father? To what extent is their influence transmitted through their genes and to what extent through the environment they provided for you?
>
> Myers 1989, p3

The link between our parents and us is always there and it affects so much of what we do in our life. When we're growing up, it is quite common to go through a phase of rebelling against our parents. We do this as part of our search for our own identity, but in order to find it we have to return to them and the family line to help us. In this section I refer to the work of Eric Berne (1964) because his studies on transactional analysis help us to understand why we are so like our parents, why we choose partners and why communication breaks down. I also draw on explanations from Margaret Hough (2014); lecturer and writer specialising in counselling.

In any given moment in our everyday adult world, Berne (1964, p23) talks about us being in an 'ego state'. This is a mental state that we are in at any time we communicate with another person. It is a mental state, which affects thought processes, attitudes, behaviour and performance and there are three ego states: Parent, Adult, and Child.

Imagine you wake up late. You rush out of the house and miss your train. You'll be late for that important meeting at work. There are different ways of reacting to this.

- The Child despairs: 'Oh no, what am I going to do? Someone help me'.
- The Critical Parent immediately thinks of someone to blame: 'That's his fault; he made me late. I'll kill him when I get home!'
- The Adult thinks: 'I'll phone someone at work and tell them there's a problem with the train; then I'll ring for a taxi'.

Looking at these three responses it is obvious that being in the Adult ego state is the most productive. Now, although we generally use all ego states at some time or other we do tend to live in one more than the others or rely on one ego state in certain situations.

*…a collection of recordings from birth to adolescence.*

## Indications of ego states

There are two types of Parent ego state: the Critical Parent (or Controlling Parent) and the Nurturing Parent. When you're in one of these states, you feel and behave in ways that you learnt from your parents, teachers or any other significant adults when you were growing up. You draw on a vast store from what you saw and heard from them. You utilise a collection of recordings from birth to adolescence. It concerns taking responsibility or taking charge of, depending on whether you are a Critical or a Nurturing Parent.

*The Critical Parent* mainly criticises and dictates. They are judgemental and moralistic. They like to let you know what they think and that they know best. They say things like 'you should know that', 'you must do that', 'that's wrong', 'you ought to know better' or 'you're fired'. Phrases that contain words such as 'should' and 'ought' are very patronising and are used in order to make someone feel inadequate. It's about having control over someone. However, they don't always have to speak to let you know they're in the Critical Parent ego state. You can tell from their posture and the way that they're looking at you. If ever you get back from work and see your partner staring at you frowning with his hands on his hips you know instantly that you've done something wrong and you're in trouble. You are the Child to his Parent state and you're going to be told off.

Think about the times you're in the Critical Parent state yourself. If you like to have control over someone else or you are constantly telling them what they should be doing then you are the Critical or Controlling Parent. It may be with your children, it may be with your friends, your colleagues, or it may even be just with your partner. On the other hand, you may know those around you who are generally in this state with you. It might be a member of your family; it could even be *your* partner. If so, you can find yourself being the Adaptive Child to compensate and make life easier.

The *Nurturing Parent* is someone who naturally protects and comforts. They show understanding of our feelings and are very caring. They want to look after us and take our troubles away. They're concerned for our feelings. They use encouraging phrases like 'I love you', 'you're doing ever so well' or 'well done'. They are accepting and friendly, loving and comforting. When we were in trouble as a child it was often the Nurturing Parent we went to first. Even now they are someone we turn to when we need reassurance and we like them around to look after us when we're ill. If we pay a lot of money to stay at a hotel we want to be surrounded by Nurturing Parents pampering to our every need.

In the *Adult* ego state you are more rational. It's a non-emotional state that uses your intelligence. You observe, collect information and evaluate the probable outcomes of situations. This part of you emerges when you first become mobile as a child: when you go out and find out things for yourself.

The *Adult* is calm and reasoning. They're interested in finding out more information and collecting the facts. They reason things out logically, they're observant and rational.

They're not someone you'd want to necessary go to a party with, but you can always guarantee that they are always the same. Think about your boss. Do you have to wait until he is in a good mood before you can talk to him? If so, then he rarely exists in the Adult ego state, which is a shame really because that's what most of us want in a good manager.

The Child ego state has two types: the Free Child and the Adaptive Child. These relate to your responses in childhood. Therefore, you feel and act typically as you did when you were growing up. You experience strong feelings and emotions, you have fun, and you adapt to or feel bad about the demands of those around you.

The *Free Child* is curious and fun loving. They want fun, they get excited and just feel free to release and show their emotions whether it's raging or laughing. They can be loud and energetic, humorous and fun, sexy and cheeky, flirtive and naughty. They are the sort of person that you *would* want to go to a party with because they bring out the Child in you. They help you to have fun without you worrying about it. They are a free spirit without restrictions. Incidentally, when you're on a romantic evening for two with your partner (or someone else for that matter), when you go into sexy mode and start flirting then you're in the Free Child ego state. There are no constraints on the Free Child.

The *Adaptive Child* struggles with the world. They either reluctantly accept and submit to the demands of those around them or they rebel. They range from being angry and fighting against everything to feeling ashamed, being compliant and apologetic. They say things like 'I can't do this', 'I'll try my best', 'I'm sorry', 'everyone's against me' or 'nobody likes me'. The voice tone is whiney and moaning. They pout or foot stamp. When they don't get their own way they make sure you know by looking dejected; in other words sulking. If you sulk, remember it's Adaptive Child behaviour. You do it because you didn't get your own way – you'll notice some football managers slip into this. You want the arbitrators to feel bad and take responsibility for the way they've made you feel. And there are those who can sulk for years. An example of this is when adults blame their parents for their up-bringing: 'if they hadn't have done that I would be …' or 'if it wasn't for that decision I could've done …'. They can't let it go and they conclude that it's the reason why they are like they are, and use it as an excuse. Sulking can be a lifetime choice that helps the individual deflect any blame away from themselves or having to accept who they are.

In a relationship, sulking can be a regular occurrence and an alternative to arguing. It's hard living with someone all the time, especially if you realise that you don't particularly like them. So instead of confronting issues, which could lead to arguing sometimes, it's easier to hide feelings and sulk. This means, of course, that the unresolved issues are seething within and often stored as ammunition ready to be unleashed when the moment calls for it. This is often done when someone feels under attack by their partner. If you do sulk, chances are you did it as a child and possibly one of your parents was also a 'sulker'.

THE INCREDIBLE SULK

'The state is produced by the playback of recorded data of events in the past, involving real people, real times, real places, real decisions, and real feelings' (Harris 1973, p18). Therefore, that's why we end up reacting in the same way our parents did. It's what we've learned and absorbed as we were growing up. It's what we know. Therefore, when we're parents ourselves, we rely on that stored information to raise our children.

To really progress as a human we need to keep in mind that 'growing up is the act of stepping from childhood into adulthood' (Scott Peck 1990, p122). However, it's not always that easy and being human means that we revert to using all of these ego states.

A good example of where these ego states can be seen is in television comedy. What makes a character funny is that they are grown up but they're acting like an 'Adaptive Child.' The comedy is brought out by them struggling to cope with being a grown-up, and that they feel the world is against them. This character is supported in most sit-coms by a 'Critical Parent' who can sometimes alternate with being a 'Nurturing Parent.' Also, there's often a 'Free Child' who's usually too naïve to be aware of any constraints that are really out there in the world, so they have no idea of any responsibilities. The 'Adult' character in a lot of comedy shows is often played by a woman and it is this that highlights the absurdity of the behaviour of the male 'Adaptive Child.' Sometimes, there's a charismatic good-looking male 'Adult', who, like in real life, combines this role with the 'Free Child.' This injects humour into the 'Adult' and makes the character very appealing. If you know anyone who is 'Adult' but who adopts a flirtive, playful side to their character, it is the combination of the 'Adult' ego state and the 'Free Child.' It's very attractive and very charismatic.

---

Using one famous comedy programme as an example to highlight these ego states is *Fawlty Towers*. Although the characters do go into other ego states they are predominately in the following:

- Basil – Adaptive Child
- Manuel and the Colonel – Free Child
- Sybil – Critical Parent
- Polly – Adult

---

As I mentioned earlier, we adopt all these ego states although we might be in one more than the others. You may assume one just for work and another at home. You might always resort to one particular state when you react in certain situations or when you feel stressed. You can automatically go into one state as a reaction to your partner's approach to you. Even as a grown up, you can go straight into the 'Adaptive Child' state as soon as you see your parents, especially if they are still quite dominant. Whichever ego state you're in then determines how you communicate with your partner.

*...Adult-to-Adult. This is where couples can talk and things can get sorted, as long as they stay there.*

## Communication

When it comes to communication between two people, the ego states play their part. When we communicate with someone we do so from one particular ego state in ourselves and direct our communication to a particular ego state in another. These are called transactions and there are three types: complementary, crossed and ulterior.

Complementary transactions – this is when the response comes from the ego state to which it was aimed and is directed back to the ego state it originated from.

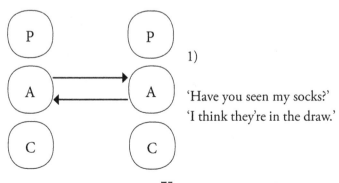

1)

'Have you seen my socks?'
'I think they're in the draw.'

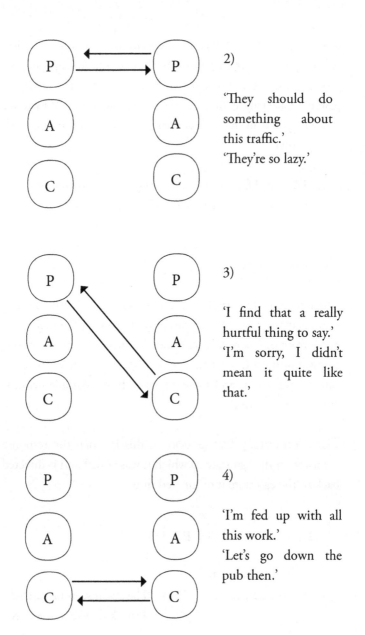

2)

'They should do something about this traffic.'
'They're so lazy.'

3)

'I find that a really hurtful thing to say.'
'I'm sorry, I didn't mean it quite like that.'

4)

'I'm fed up with all this work.'
'Let's go down the pub then.'

With all these examples the response came from the ego state to which it was targeted. In the second example both 'Critical Parents' just wanted to have a moan and have someone to blame and so both responded complementary. They got the response they wanted. When you want to have a moan you look for someone who will also want to do the same. In the third example the 'Critical Parent' tells off an 'Adaptive Child', but because the response was from the 'Child' saying 'sorry,' it defused the situation. That's what often happens when someone apologises, it's difficult then for the other person to keep on at them, because they've disarmed them by taking full responsibility. In other words, they've responded from the ego state to which the other directed it. In the fourth example whenever there's talk of going down to the pub, it's always from the 'Free Child' ego state, because it's essentially about not worrying about things. The pub is a form of escapism. Obviously, the most productive, as regards two people talking, is 'Adult-to-Adult.' This is where couples can talk and things can get sorted, as long as they stay there. In this 'Adult-to-Adult' transaction, both can talk freely without fear that the other will get upset, go in a mood, attack or sulk. Both stay rational and receptive to the other. Unfortunately, when a relationship is not right this 'Adult-to-Adult' state is not operational for long enough.

Crossed transactions – this is when the sender does not get the desired results. He or she aims the transaction at one ego state, but gets a response from another. In situations like these communication breaks down.

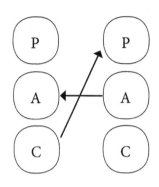

1)

'Hello love, I've had an awful day.'
'I see the squirells have taken all the nuts again.'

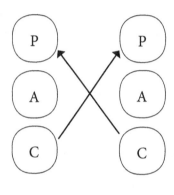

2)

'I've had a rough day today.'
'You're not the only one to work hard you know.'

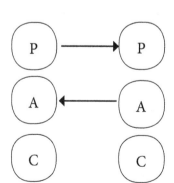

3)

'Have you heard the gossip about Joan next door?'
'I don't think we should be talking about that until she's said something herself.'

In the first example, all you wanted was a 'Nurturing Parent,' but you've been cut dead by a non-emotional response from the 'Adult.' You've not been heard and it definitely wasn't the response you wanted. In the second example, you end up thinking 'where the hell did that come from?' Those who always take things personally tend to respond from the 'Adaptive Child' or 'Critical Parent' ego state because they are defending themselves. They do this by attacking. That's why, when you're having an adult to adult discussion with your partner and they suddenly react to something you've said, they respond from another ego state. The discussion is really at an end until you both get back to adult to adult. Partners can switch ego state very quickly and sometimes you just have to wait until they come back. In the third example, you're all ready for a bit of gossip and then someone ends up going completely rational on you. You then feel bad for even contemplating delving into a bit of scandal.

*...we hide behind flirting because we can always deny our intent if we are challenged*

In all the examples, the conversation is stopped and until it gets back to a complementary transaction communication can do nothing else but break down.

Ulterior transactions – these are used when a psychological game is being played: to say one thing while intent on meaning something quite different. This happens a lot in relationships.

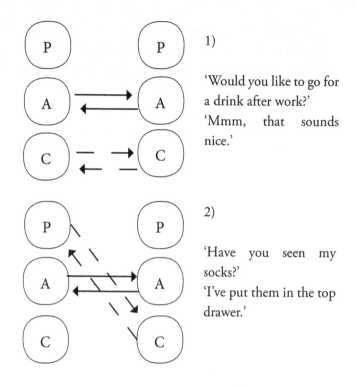

1)

'Would you like to go for a drink after work?'
'Mmm, that sounds nice.'

2)

'Have you seen my socks?'
'I've put them in the top drawer.'

With example one, if we fancy someone we can't really just go up to them and say 'look, I find you so attractive and I would really like to go to bed with you' (even though in reality that's what we want when we do fancy someone). To do so would leave us too exposed and vulnerable (not that I've ever tried it). What if they laugh in my face? What if they just want to be friends? What if they give me a smack? What if they report me for sexual harassment? Instead we have to play a game and work our way around someone until we're more certain that we won't be rejected. Self-esteem can be very fragile for most of us. Therefore, we hide behind flirting because we can always deny our intent if we're challenged.

The second example is more common in relationships. In this instance what is being said has nothing to do with what is actually meant. The real dialogue, or the sub text, might be:

- 'Why are you always moving my clothes?'
- 'Why am I always having to tidy up after you?'

Or

- 
- 'Why can't you just leave things where I left them?'
- 'Why are you always criticising me?'

By using these ulterior transactions it avoids any confrontation. There are also other times when we don't really want to say how we really feel, so we use different words to disguise what we really mean. For example:

- 'You know Colin in Accounts, he's only gone and got the dates mixed up and come in today in fancy dress ... *bless him*!'

Or

- 'I don't know how he did it but Mr Davies down the road has managed to lock himself in his own shed again ... *bless*!'

In most cases, whenever we say *bless* or *bless him* in circumstances such as these at the end of a sentence when talking about something stupid someone has done, (it's usually a man) what we really mean is *fucking idiot*. We don't say *fucking idiot* because that indicates that we're being too much of a 'Critical

Parent' and it can sound too unkind, even when we might say it under our breath. So, we replace it with *bless* or *bless him,* but realistically the meaning is just the same.

- 'Mr Brown across the road is watering his garden …in the rain …*bless!*'
- 'Mr Brown across the road is watering his garden …in the rain …*fucking idiot!*'

- 'You know Pete in the office next door has got his trousers on back to front …*bless him!*'
- 'You know Pete in the office next door has got his trousers on back to front …*fucking idiot!*'

Saying *bless* is just a softer way of voicing our criticism. However, this only applies to adults and not when we are talking about children or animals.

What all this means is that the meaning of what someone says isn't in the actual words that they use: it's in the person themselves. Couples play the ulterior transaction game to hide what they really mean, because otherwise it would cause confrontation. If you are at a stage where most of your conversations with your partner are like this nothing can be achieved until you both get back to an 'Adult-to-Adult' complementary transaction.

Another conclusion to all this, of course, is that no one can make you feel something. Have you ever said something like 'he makes me angry when he says that', 'she always gets me mad', or 'I've only got to see her and I'm agitated'? The truth is that your reaction is a choice as no one can make you feel these things. They can invite you to be angry or sad, but whether you choose to be is up to you. They can direct something to a particular ego state in you, but whether you respond from that ego state is your choice. In normal circumstances, the idea that someone can't help behaving in a certain way is nonsense. To say otherwise indicates that others have complete control over someone else's internal make up. As O'Connor and Seymour (1993, p103) point out 'one person does not have direct control over another person's emotional state'.

This all demonstrates that a lot of conversations between couples are based on the ulterior transaction. For communication to develop between them, the only way is for both to converse at the 'Adult-to-Adult' ego state and stay there. Once you communicate out of this state the conversation is really over and you both need to get it back.

*…the average marriage contract is made by the child…*

# Ego states and choosing a partner

Berne (1964) identified that we can get stuck in parts of our personality by resorting to a particular ego state. Skynner and Cleese (1993b) add to this by saying 'if we want to be dependent and irresponsible, or frightened of sex, we can use the child-like parts of ourselves; so we avoid developing the more grown up responsible aspects of ourselves – even to the point of denying we have them in us' (p58). They go on to suggest that if someone spends most of their life in one of these ego states while closing down the other parts to their personality, they function at a lower level. The reason for this is that they're not using all the resources needed to cope with life.

When someone chooses a partner it can often be done to complement his or her own ego state. For example, a person who predominately exists in a 'Child' ego state will look towards someone who can look after them; while a 'Nurturing Parent' will want someone to look after. They'll be drawn towards a person who can make the relationship more of a balance; hence, why some choose a partner who we may see as totally immature and unsuitable. For example,

> …someone operating mainly through the child part of themselves – an alcoholic for example – will seek out a so-called 'rescuer' – someone who is uncomfortable with being dependent and has therefore denied the child-like part of themselves. And the rescuer needs the contact with the child-like person, in order to cope with their denied dependence by dealing with it vicariously! To put it another way, each needs someone else to

'carry' the part of themselves they are uncomfortable with, and want to avoid by off-loading it ...couples like this will find it impossible to feel emotionally independent of one another.

Skynner and Cleese 1993b, pp59-60

Most marriages take place when the couple are in the phase of being in love. In the context of Berne's work '...the average marriage contract is made by the child, which understands love as something you feel and not something you do, and which sees happiness as something you pursue rather than a by-product of working towards the happiness of someone other than yourself' (Harris 1973, p124).

This brings me back to the point I made in chapter two where couples, particularly women, talk only about the wedding day which is, essentially, about being the centre of attention. It is a very special day and that's why people spend months planning things down to the minutest detail, but they rarely speak of their feelings towards their partner or how life will be after they are married. In circumstances such as these, there's almost a disconnection towards their relationship before the marriage, which has the possibility to continue and widen after the big day. As the 'Adult' is missing in most of the decision making for many couples at this stage, there is more of a reliance and dependence on the romantic idea as seen through books and films.

As this chapter has identified, it is the way that we learnt or didn't learn stages of development in our childhood that has determined a lot of our behaviour as an adult. It has also influenced us unconsciously in the way we choose someone to be our partner. You might have got that right but there will be many reading this book that feel that they did not. How we dealt with these stages can also determine the ego states we adopt now. An understanding of these can reveal why communication between our partner and ourselves often breaks down. To finish the chapter, I think it's worth sex and relationship expert and author Suzi Godson (2011, p7) having the final word on this:

> When two people start a relationship they take with them a predictable, almost universal, set of hopes and aspirations, which usually includes the dream of a happy ending. In reality, the minute they form a couple they begin to create their own unique narrative, a script which is driven by their personalities, their experiences, their sexual history and more often than not the trolley of monogrammed emotional baggage that they have each dragged into the relationship.

# Part Two

So far I've tried to determine how we assess our own normality. I've looked at relationships and the concept of love and why relationships are so very important to us. I've examined how we choose a partner and why communication can break down so easily. From this you may have thought of some ideas regarding developing your own relationship. However, before you go making any plans it would be useful to familiarise yourself with how men think.

In the second part of the book, I focus more on the physical side of your relationship and what can be done about it. How does a man think and is it normal? How does he come to think about you and your relationship with him? How does he think when it comes to sex? You need to have a glimpse into the way his mind works in order to understand what you're dealing with, because only then can you start to have some sort of influence. I finish the section with three chapters for your man to read. Some of it might be uncomfortable reading so read them first and then it's up to you to devise a way to get your partner to read them.

In the next chapter, I focus on how men think and their attitude toward sex. You may not like, it but it would be useful to know. I explain why they are better at thinking about sex than actually doing it. I tell you a secret that they have about you and the truth about make-up. I tell you why you don't want to be spending a lot of time choosing certain jewellery to wear, and what you can wear that he will really notice. I explain the way his mind works when he sees other women and the system he uses to categorise them. I clarify how we all escape to a fantasy world at times and why it's necessary. I conclude by identifying who he is really communicating with when he's with all his mates and an attractive woman passes by.

# Chapter Five

*How men think and what they think about*

In this chapter I cover:
- How men think about sex and what they like.
- The truth about make-up and earrings.
- The world of fantasy he lives in.
- Why men look at porn.
- What men think of during and after sex.
- How behaviour changes when men are with their mates.

I must point out at this stage that men are not all the same. There are those who behave in honourable ways and never have any carnal thoughts about anyone other than their wife. But then again I could be wrong. Maybe it's just that they don't show it.

*… it's often the thought of it that they can manage better than actually doing it.*

## Understanding how men think

Some of you will already have a good understanding of the workings of the male mind. You might have read books such as *Men and Other Primates* or *Getting to Know Your Penis* and gained an understanding of men (actually the books don't exist; I just made them up). You may have found out what men are like through your own experience. You might, for example, already be on your third husband. If you are, this can look more like a hobby and the fact that you are reading this book may suggest that you're probably on the look-out for number four. If you've already bought your current husband the T shirt with 'No 3' on it, he may be sensing his number is almost up.

Let's face it – men adore sex. But it's often the thought of it that they can manage better than actually doing it. Men see themselves as great lovers, but like a lot of things it's mainly in their head and based on their own criteria. Apparently there is research that suggests that men think about sex every few seconds. I don't doubt this at all; I'm just not sure how it's measured. Also, it raises the question as to what they are thinking about the rest of the time. The fact remains that his penis can have quite an influence over his life and can contribute to some of his more significant decisions. It can have a mind of its own. Think about first thing in the morning: it even gets up before he does. Have you ever wondered why he waits a few minutes before he makes you a cup of tea? He's waiting for it to go down. It can be very embarrassing when he gets up with that thing protruding from his Sponge Bob pyjamas and then bumping into your mother in the kitchen.

## A design flaw

The female body does something to most of us. It has the power to make us go all-weak. Whether you like it or not we get attracted to trashy. It makes our heads turn. Remember the film *Grease*? Danny only became really interested when Sandy wore that black, skin-tight, tarty outfit and high heels – talk about a love story! We also adore low-cut tops that show off a cleavage. It's immaterial whose cleavage it belongs to – we can't help but look. We can notice one from 100 yards away, even without our glasses on. It's like a magnet. I know you've had men speak to you while the entire time they stare at your cleavage. That's bad! Some men don't have any awareness of what they're doing. At least the courteous ones will wait until you're not looking before they inspect your cleavage – that's surely the decent thing to do! Today's push-up bras just bring out the beauty in cleavages even more and enhance the figure – you don't need me to tell you that; even women look at other women. We also know when you're not wearing one. We sense it. Whereas you have 'female' intuition we have 'not wearing a bra' intuition. There's no escaping the fact that men love boobs – all shapes and sizes. You see we haven't got any ourselves (well, most of us haven't) and anything we haven't got ignites our fascination.

Here's a little secret for you about your boobs. It's normal for him to have a favourite one. It might be the slightly bigger one because, as you've always known even from a very early age, one is always slightly larger than the other. He'll obviously treat them both the same because he wouldn't want the less favoured one to feel left out (not in today's equal opportunities society). However, he can't help it, he does like one more than the other. That's the dilemma when there's always two of something. I know that you don't have a favourite testicle, but, believe it or not, he might. Some men have one where the inside ball occasionally pops out and therefore has to be pushed back in – this can be very uncomfortable, especially at intimate moments.

There are not that many men that like false boobs, not even in an emergency, especially if they don't wobble. And although men always notice women with big boobs the general rule is that anything above a handful is a bit unmanageable; however, it is very much a personal thing. And as for gigantic false boobs, they can tend to look more like a health and safety issue.

*...you are wasting your time wearing them for us.*

## Long hair, make-up and earrings

We do tend to also like long hair, although it's not always essential. We don't mind straight or curly, but we're not keen when it's in curlers – that can be quite a scary look. The main point is that generally we only like hair on your head. We're not keen on it sprouting elsewhere, especially the armpits, but even you don't like it growing there. I've heard the argument that this idea of hairless bodies has evolved from Internet porn and it's probably true, but like any advertising, it drags us in and creates our tastes for us.

Another thing you may be interested in is the myth about make-up. We tend not to like too much of it, especially when we're in a relationship with you. We prefer subtle. It's especially awful with stuff like foundation when the colour on your face ends up being different to the rest of your body. Young girls use make-up to look older and the rest use it to look younger. Essentially, women apply it to look nice and although we do notice, we prefer less. It can't be good for your skin and therefore you may regret it later on. There does appear to be a lot of young, very attractive women about looking like they've been using products from the *Ronseal* outdoor weather-proof range, when in actual fact they don't need to use much make-up, if any at all. Some of them must be getting up in the middle of the night to get ready for work. Less is more. It's the same with fake tans. So often it just doesn't look natural. It also damages the skin and gives off that radioactive look.

As regards to jewellery, and in particular earrings, I don't really want to disappoint you but we generally don't notice them. Ask your husband what earrings you wore last night and I'm betting he's going to have an educated guess. They're useful to us because it helps us buy you presents when we're stuck for ideas, but after that we have no memory of which ones we've brought you. We're more likely to have your cleavage imprinted on our mind, so unless you've worn earrings that are big and dominant there's really no way we will remember them. This means, of course, that you are wasting your time wearing them for us. In fact, you're really wearing them for yourself and other women. You see it's other women who are much more likely to notice them than us.

## Shoes

You probably know what I'm going to say here. When it comes to shoes, men love high heels, especially black ones, they make most legs look great. We don't know how you walk in them, but we're not too worried about that. Anything with some sort of heel is fine by us, especially boots. Put them with a short-ish skirt and we're melting. We'd quite happily follow a short skirt and high heels all the way to work even though we're supposed to be going in the opposite direction. For us, it's very much based on the visual. That's why we like to make love with the lights blazing and with your shoes on. It's the one time we're unconcerned about the electricity bill or being stabbed in the leg by your heel.


## Sexy but subtle

Men tend to like stockings, especially when they're black and, of course, when you've got your legs inside them. And we adore fishnets. It's just that tights are not sexy. We know why you wear them and those of us who wear 'Long Johns' can't really complain because we wear them for the same practical reasons. But they are not sexy – and neither are Long Johns. We like skimpy pants, corsets and basques. Unfortunately, a lot of basques seem to have about 240 buttons or hooks on them to undo. By the time we've undone all of those we've missed *Match of the Day* – thank goodness for Velcro. We don't go for the 'love me for my mind' outfits in the bedroom. We prefer skimpy things such as see-through nighties and that wet, shiny, plastic latex look you can't breathe in properly. With clothing, we like it revealing so that we can use our imagination. We relish subtle because our brains have to do some of the work. We even like tassels. It all adds to the mystery of what's underneath, we delight in the tease of unwrapping you. Of course, we're always fond of naked and we'll always look at pictures of naked women, but that's just the design flaw within us.

I'm not going to mention anything about body shape. I know the media and the fashion industry have influenced us all to feel inadequate for not being skinny, but not all of us like skinny. It's very much down to personal preference.

*Fantasies are a form of escapism and everyone has them.*

## Fantasy

Men are always looking at women and asking themselves 'would I?' If there's a photograph on the office wall of everyone in the department chances are he'll be scanning it counting which ones he'd like to get intimate with. When he passes women in the street he's categorising them into either 'yes, I would' or 'no, I wouldn't'. Or there might be more categories in his system:

- definitely,
- maybe under certain circumstances,
- no, I don't think so at this stage,
- definitely not under any circumstances.

It's a fantasy world and it's not worth you quizzing him about it, he'll only deny it. Men know what you want to hear unless they're really stupid. Fantasies are a form of escapism and everyone has them. It's the way his mind works. It might even be the way your mind works, but probably in a slightly different way – although I can't be sure of that.

Think of the fantasies you have. You'll notice that they exist in a perfect world. Nothing ever goes wrong in them. If they did come true then there would be all sorts of problems you would have to deal with. Reality has a habit of bringing negative factors to the surface. Fantasies are reality avoidance: you don't get hurt, you always enjoy yourself and you never catch anything that you might be ashamed of. For men, they have the Internet. They visit porn sites and satisfy themselves while they're on there. Porn is a fantasy world. It's safe sex for men. They don't have to worry about leering at someone, making sure they're all right and satisfying them. And as soon as the happy ending occurs everybody goes home.

Although men like to look at women on the Internet and in glossy magazines, surprisingly, they are not so attracted to top models. If you look at the women in the *Ann Summers* catalogue you'll probably find that most men perceive them to be unattainable. They prefer naughty pictures of 'readers' wives', where a woman looks friendly and fun; someone who looks like they would enjoy the physical side of a relationship, someone they would feel comfortable with – not someone pouting and looking uncompromising.

> Sexual fantasy is a private opportunity to explore the sex you will never have with people who will never have you. It's escapism, a fast-forward to arousal, and the general consensus among therapists is that it is harmless as long as it doesn't become obsessive or put anyone at risk.
>
> Godson 2011, p74

*...don't expect him to admit it to you.*

## Fantasy during sex

For some men, performing (when I say performing I don't mean juggling or something like that to entertain you) in the bedroom with images of what they've seen on the porn site in their head can help them to keep going. They may even be thinking of past partners. As I said to you before, don't go asking him about things like this. For a start 'men can't even admit to themselves that they fantasize about someone else when they are having sex' (Godson 2011, p73), so don't expect him to admit it to you. Also, he would never think to ask you what you think about during sex and if he did I doubt very much whether you would tell him. We can't help being sexual creatures, we can't help but think about other women in bed; it's just the way we're built. And don't say 'my husband isn't like that'! I've heard women say 'yes, I know men are like that but my dear old dad wasn't!' Unfortunately, even if he was devoted to your mother, helped with the housework, always volunteered on charity days and was a Morris Dancer in his spare time – he would've if he could've!

Apart from fantasising about sex during sex, the other thing you should probably know is that the moment he has come (and I mean that as a sexual term rather than him coming round to your house), once the deed is done and you're both lying there sticking to each other, frantically stretching in unnatural positions in order to reach the tissues without anything falling out and making even more mess, he's probably already thinking about football again. It could even be *Top Gear* or what's for tea. I don't know about women and what their immediate thoughts are, maybe it's *Britain's Got Talent* or why the wet patch is always on her side of the bed. Unfortunately, I do fear that, for many women, these thoughts may well pop into their head long before they start soaking up that first tissue.

## Men – thinking of sex even on the first date

On your first date he might actually be interested in the Arts or what your hobbies are, but it's not his first thought. The first date is a strange one. Of course he'd like you to go to bed with him, but strangely enough he'll be keener on you if you don't. Men want what they can't have and it keeps them interested. If you flirt with him and he believes he can't have you it will drive him crazy. If he knows he's going to have sex with you the challenge isn't there and men do like a challenge. We don't appreciate things that come easy to us; that's why we crave what we can't reach.

Going to bed with someone for the first time can be quite awkward because the relationship is rarely at a stage where sex can be discussed openly. In reality, a lot of men don't really know how to satisfy a woman, as they are generally more concerned about their own pleasure. As many have not learnt how to deal with adult situations, they pretend that they know what they're doing (as referred to in chapter four). Therefore, they rely on the little knowledge they have. The difficulty with new relationships is that he has tended to have had a longer and closer bond with his right hand than with any woman. In a way this is your competition.

How men think is quite straightforward when it comes to sex, but you've probably seen how it is all accentuated and exaggerated when they are with their mates. They seem to change personality.

*...they are sending the signals back to their male counterparts...*

## Men in groups

For women it can be an intimidating situation when they walk past a group of boys or men in a jovial mood trying to show off to each other. Their whole personality can change, as they appear to slide down the evolutionary scale. They leer and grunt as if it's an aphrodisiac formula to attract women. 'I'd give her one!'; 'get 'em out for the lads!' It just seems strange that any ability to think logically flies out of the window. The reason for this is that confidence grows when humans are surrounded and protected by others around them. In fact, in order for us to feel accepted we have to adhere to the rituals, behaviours and norms of the group. It can be really difficult to go against this consensus when self-esteem or self-respect hasn't yet flourished within us. Being in a group shields us from our own anxieties of being accepted. This is why youngsters start imitating those around them who are perhaps older and appear more self-confident. It is often the reason why smoking, drinking or taking drugs starts at such an early age (although they might be put off these activities if they read chapter seven). As men get older and progress into more adult pastimes, it's certainly the reason why they brag about sexual conquests and tell dirty jokes.

Men in groups wolf-whistle women, look them up and down as they walk by, mentally undress them and send out 'Neanderthal' grunts. In a way, they're not communicating with the woman herself, rather they are sending the signals back to their male counterparts as a sign that they are one of them. For women, it's bad enough being subjected to this sort of intimidating and harassing behaviour but many have said that not receiving it can make them feel that they are no longer attractive enough to even get a reaction. You just can't win!

So men in groups can be quite frightening, but a relatively new phenomenon that has emerged during the last few decades is women in groups: in particular – hen parties.

Again, individuals in groups tend to develop confidence and behave in ways they would never dream of if they were on their own. There's freedom in a group along with security. In such situations, there also seems to be some sort of volume control, which gets louder and louder as the evening goes on. For those of us out for a quiet drink it's almost worth staying in on a Friday night.

As I've highlighted in this chapter, his thoughts are never far from sex. Whether you like it or not, it's quite normal with men. He thinks about it a lot and what he likes you to wear can be quite predictable. However, the fantasy world he lives in and the education he's received regarding all things carnal, may not have prepared him that well to please you in the bedroom. He now needs further educating and that's where you come in. But before you start, there's something very important you need to know. This I discuss in the next chapter. I explain that sex doesn't always have to be about penetration and how you need to send him signals to indicate he's pleasing you. If you want to enjoy sex more than you do currently then read on.

# Chapter Six

*Train your man in the bedroom*

In this chapter I cover:
- Knowing what you like before you start any training.
- How a man relies on your guidance and instruction.
- How men learn about sex.
- Feeling comfortable about what you do in the bedroom.
- Learning what he likes.


Whether you've been with your partner a long time, or just in the early stages of a relationship, you may have an ideal picture of how you want the relationship to flourish and develop. This means you're going to have to work at it and if you want the physical side to be more enjoyable then you're going to have to train your man. I don't mean in the sense of controlling him in everything he does, but if you want him to do the right things in the bedroom he needs guidance as to what to do. First of all, he's got to understand that the clitoris isn't a Greek island somewhere near cunnilingus (Russell 1989). You might be saying 'well, he should know what to do by now', or 'I've dropped enough hints'. The truth is that men generally are not good at psychic or subtle. We need to have it in clear simple language. We can spend years trying to work out your coded messages and sophisticated hints in order to guess what you really meant by something – no wonder our hair falls out.

Therefore, you've got to be clear and use precise instructions when you tell us. But before you do that there's something else you have to do.

## Know what you like

You've got to know what you like. What I mean by this is realising what your realistic romantic fantasies are, how you want your man to treat you and how you would like to be touched. It's complicated because in most romantic novels and films the man seems to know what to do. He doesn't need to be told. And if he doesn't know, then by the end of the film he'll have the ability to work it out through reflection. Unfortunately, in real life not many of us are really like that and so could do with some help. What I mean here is emotionally in our relationship and physically in the bedroom.

In the bedroom, you've got to know what turns you on. What are your daydreams made of and, more importantly, what do you do on your own when you're satisfying yourself? Only you know the answer to this. When it comes to orgasms, most of us, both men and women, are better at doing it ourselves, because of the practice we've had. You know what you like: whether you prefer fast or slow motion, circular or up and down, firm or light, two hands or just one. If you like just one hand you know full well what the other hand is up to at the same time. Think about where you touch yourself. Do you use a sex toy inside at the same time or a vibrator on your clitoris? You need to know how long you prefer it to last and how often you do it. Do you prefer to masturbate in the morning or when you go to bed? You might feel uncomfortable reading this and mentally answering these questions, but knowing this stuff is important before you invite someone to join in. You need to know yourself first.

Only you know what you think about when you do it. Keep in mind that there are two types of fantasies here. There are those which you may dream of but you probably wouldn't want to come true. I say this because you wouldn't have enough control over the situation. I'm thinking of S & M and perhaps other stuff you may have read about in books such as *Fifty Shades of Grey*. Then there are the other fantasies, which are more realistic: the sort that results in ultimate romantic satisfaction, the gentle affection you crave for which someone could potentially fulfil, given the training.

It's quite easy for women to turn us on. Most of us are built to the same specification. You've only got to take your top off and we're panting. It's relatively straight forward bringing a man to orgasm and many women have done it without actually knowing too much about it. We are quite easily pleased, and a lot of us are more than happy that we have someone to actually do it with. On the other hand, women tend to be different with more of a variety of individual needs and desires than men, it's just they weren't included in our education.

*We tend not to like the idea of our parents having sex and enjoying it at the same time.*

## How men learn about sex

Your man needs training because chances are his education derived from girly magazines and porn sites. This may well have started in his childhood and he's more than likely made a career out of it. The education he received at school was probably more about reproduction rather than anything to do with the sensual side of satisfying a woman. It's doubtful that the pleasures and the feelings associated with sex were ever mentioned in classes. For me, I remember it tended to be quite formal with reference to how flowers pollinate. All this seemed to be in cartoon form with arrows pointing to the various parts of the body as if it were a map of the inland waterways. It can't be easy to teach sex in schools with class sizes of over 30 all giggling at every sex-related reference.

Another source of sex education comes from our parents, which, unfortunately, means that for many of us we may not have received any at all. We tend not to like the idea of our parents having sex and enjoying it at the same time. We like to see it as a later invention within our own generation. The thought of our parents telling us what goes where and when and using words such as erection, orgasm, ejaculation, and mutual masturbation could possibly take years of therapy to get over. As for oral sex, let's just not go there!

This ultimately means that the sources of education are limited. There's a big gap and yet it's one of the most influential topics in our lives. We see it everywhere and ideally most of us would like to be reasonably good at it as well as enjoy it.

All this means, of course, is that you as a woman have to take the lead to make up for his lack of education. He now needs the training. He's got to realise that women are not like the ones on the porn site and that sex isn't just about his own gratification. The only way to do this is by talking to him intimately, which means you've got to know what you personally like first before you start.

## Train your man

Explore what you do like and, in your mind, work out how to delegate these tasks to your man. Don't expect him to know. You could, of course, paint an arrow on yourself pointing to the clitoris but chances are he still wouldn't find it. Sometimes they seem to move about. They're not always in the same place they seemed to be yesterday. Fortunately they do seem to be bigger these days than they used to be – that's healthy eating for you!

You need to tell him what you like and what gets you tingling. Most of us get a kick out of turning someone on. If we know we're good at something it becomes really important to us and is the starting point of giving rather than taking in the bedroom. You need to show him where to touch you, how to touch you, and how to bring you to ecstasy; otherwise he'll just assume your satisfaction is through penetration and penetration only. It might be, but it's doubtful. Chances are there are other things that you would like him to successfully perform. If he's trying to make you come, then you need to guide him about the hand pressure and coach him as to the rhythm. Keep in mind that he may not be ambidextrous (not amphibious; don't get those two mixed up, it could have horrifying consequences), so don't assume, for example, that he can perform the same skills on either side of the bed.

Do you like being touched and kissed at the same time? If so, then he needs to know. He can't be allowed to assume that the way he physically likes sex is how you like it.

*Remember – you can't help the way you feel.*

## Doing what you feel comfortable doing

If you do have sex and he does go inside you then you've got to get him to practice his rhythm. If need be you have got to tell him to slow down and stimulate you at the same time. If he's got satellite navigation in his car he'll be used to taking instructions. At the same time, you've also got to give off signals that he's doing the right things. Don't enjoy yourself in silence: he needs to hear you, this is very important. He needs to know that you are reaching orgasm and what he's doing is pleasing you. Under no circumstance should you be giving off these sounds when it's doing nothing for you, otherwise he'll just carry on. During and afterwards a man needs your praise. If he gets it, he'll try even harder to get more, you can't lose.

There are, of course, those who like the idea of trying out sex in holes that are ill-designed for the purpose. If you're not keen on these then you're going to have to tell him. If you do things that you don't like, then it can put you off the whole intimate part of your relationship and then it's difficult to get it back. Remember, you can't help the way you feel. The trouble is that he's seen all sorts of activities on his porn site and may be conditioned to believe that this is normal behaviour and everyone likes it. This is likely to get worse in the future as one in three children are now accessing online porn by the age of ten, so by the time they are ready for sex they draw on what they've seen. This is quite understandable when so much learning in our childhood is about copying and mimicking the behaviour of others. I know that in many relationships it's about choosing your battles but if the idea of something like anal sex turns your stomach then he's got to know as soon as possible. If you're really not sure whether to try something he has suggested, my first reaction would be to recommend you don't; not without finding out more about it first. Get hold of a copy of *Sex Counsel* by Suzi Godson; you may be able to identify with some of the questions she receives from women, and men, and this may help you to determine what you should do. You've always got to feel comfortable about what you're doing.

*If you're fantasising about sex and he's only thinking about cake then there's a real problem.*

Once he starts getting things right, then you can enhance the mood by wearing something that you know turns him on. I know some women don't like dressing up because it usually means dressing up as a tart. Unfortunately, one of you in the relationship likes tarty. Dressing up can be fun and so you may need to take a different perspective about it. It can make you feel sexy and make you feel desirable. It's a nice feeling being able to turn your man on just by walking in the room and sensing the desire he has for you. Whereas, looking like the contents of the washing basket isn't going to do much for either of you.

If you do feel a little embarrassed about your body, as most people do, subtle lighting will help. Tell him that you don't want the spot light on you as if you've been dragged in for questioning. Allow yourself time to build up your confidence because it's only this that allows you to let yourself go and feel a sense of freedom to experiment.

Of course, if you are training him to pleasure you then you should be interested in what he likes. Don't assume. Is there anywhere he likes to be touched or anywhere where he doesn't? For example, some men don't like their balls played with because it's such a sensitive area; whereas, others seem to go for a bit of rough treatment. Find out how he likes to be played with. The best way to learn is to watch how he handles himself. There's years of experience there so observe how he does it and don't be afraid to ask him to show you (but don't sit there with a pencil and notepad). As Godson (2011) identifies, the Y-shaped ridge at the head of the penis is the most sensitive area so you can't go far wrong if you focus on that; keeping in mind that it's usually better with some lubrication. There's always room for lubrication in whatever you do, it just makes everything slide together so much easier. However, make sure you get one designed for the job (not WD40). Does he like you sitting up as you do it or lying down cuddling him? Chances are he likes it all sorts of ways so you've got to help him feel at ease about telling you. This might mean practicing a 'flirtive' look or at least a smile that makes him believe you are enjoying yourself too. Don't start looking at your watch or checking your texts.

It's not easy any of this, I do know that. It's probably less of an ordeal to train a newcomer (no pun intended). For many, it's going to take quite a bit of initiative, but if you want to be happy in the bedroom, you've got to do something. It's probably much harder for those of you who have been with your partner for a long time and don't have the inclination to really want to develop the physical side. You probably hide this book where he won't see it and only get it out when he's not around, perhaps because you don't want him to see you taking an interest, it's just not worth it!

On the other hand, you may not have had sex for months, or even years. You might have tried to do it, but he regularly struggles to maintain an erection and so everything just ends up deflated. It leaves you both upset, not knowing what to say. You might be at the stage where to avoid that feeling, you don't even attempt it. If you're fantasising about sex and he's only thinking about cake then there's a real problem. This I look at in the next chapter (no, not the cake bit). I look at the possible reasons why he suffers from impotence and give you some ideas, as part of your training programme for him, to get your man back in action.

# Chapter Seven

*How to deal with your man who doesn't want to,
or can't, have sex with you*

In this chapter I cover:

- Why men can still be interested in sex without wanting to
  do it with you.
- The causes of impotence and the feelings associated with
  it.
- How to go about it if your man suffers from it.

> There is a wealth of evidence to support the link between
> sexual dissatisfaction and unhappy relationships.
> Several studies have shown that partners' experiences of
> unresolved conflicts, not feeling loved and emotional
> distance are associated with lower sexual satisfaction.
>
> Godson 2011, p157

There can be many reasons why you and your partner don't
have sex. It might be that you've just drifted apart, you
just haven't had time to do it for so long that it now feels
awkward or the relationship seems to have changed. Perhaps
you've been together a long time and he finds having sex a real
struggle. Getting older doesn't stop men thinking about sex,
but parts of his anatomy have other ideas. Apparently 'fifty
is a good age, because when a woman says, "Yes", you are

flattered, and when she says, "No", you are relieved' (Lodge 1992, pp218-219).

*...saying it's alright doesn't really help much...*

## Some men like sex; they just can't do it

You might find that your man visits porn sites more often than he changes his underwear, but he doesn't actually have sex with you. This could be because you always want to do it when the match is on, or your mother always seems to phone you at that time and you always answer it, or it could be that he suffers from erectile dysfunction – impotence as it is more commonly known. Stress, depression and exhaustion can often be causes of this, but it has also been linked with high blood pressure, diabetes and obesity. Other related causes include excessive drinking, taking recreational drugs and even smoking, which if that isn't enough to put youngsters off taking up any of these pastimes, I don't know what is. If impotence is related to any of these problems I suggest one or both of you see your GP. On the other hand, as in a lot of cases, it might be psychological and stem from the anxiety of satisfying you. This is the focus here.

If he has problems in maintaining an erection, trying to comfort him by saying 'it's all right' doesn't really help much because he still feels ashamed and inadequate. It creates anxiety and this builds and builds the longer it goes on. Sex then becomes something to fear as his mind deals with the pressure to perform. This pressure may not be coming from you but from the expectations he has in himself. This is in stark contrast to the fantasy-land of the porn site where he never disappoints anyone. When he's with you, his mind gets flooded with self-doubt. 'Am I going to satisfy her?' 'Is it going to stay up long enough?' 'Can I stop my mind from wondering?' 'Will that image of her mother on the toilet ever leave me?' 'As many men know, fear that the penis may not work probably almost guarantees that it won't' (Jenner 2010, p147). It's just easier not to get into the situation, it's easier not to do it. And if he uses condoms the pressure is more than doubled.

The problem is that the ability to perform is often all in the mind, as contemporary novelist Nick Hornby shows us in this extract from *High Fidelity* (2000, pp93-94).

Why is failure the first thing I think of when I find myself in this sort of situation? Why can't I just enjoy myself? But if you have to ask the question, then you know you're lost: self-consciousness is a man's worst enemy. Already I'm wondering whether she's as aware of my erection as I am, and if she is what she feels about it; but I can't even maintain that worry, let alone anything else, because so many other worries are crowding it out, and the next stage looks intimidatingly difficult, unfathomably terrifying, absolutely impossible.

Look at all the things that can go wrong for men. There's the nothing-happening-at-all problem, the too-much-happening-too-soon problem, the dismal-droop-after-a-promising-beginning problem, there's the size-doesn't-matter-except-in-my-case problem, the failing-to deliver-the-goods problem...

Not being able to have sex because of the anxiety involved is more common than many think, it's just not spoken about and therefore not dealt with. Most men wouldn't dream of seeking help, let alone tell their mates because of the embarrassment they feel. Some deal with it by telling you it's just a phase they're going through; others write to sex experts because of the anonymity associated with it. Take this letter for example:

> I'm a rich, OK-looking, 40-ish alpha male, yet I'm lonely. Every time I'm in bed with a woman I feel sick with nerves and can't get it up.
>
> Godson 2011, p16

With men thinking and feeling like this, it's little wonder that they fantasise and think about what they've seen on the porn site during moments of intimacy with you: anything which can help them to get it up and stay up. It stems from the thought of not wanting to let you down and the expectations they have in themselves of being a man. Our super-heroes on the big screen don't help either, as they've never suffered with this. We've never seen James Bond having to apologise and then sit in awkward silence as the girl next to him gets her knitting out.

## What to do if your man suffers from impotence

If your partner does struggle to get an erection, it's going to take time and you've both got to be patient. Therefore, without giving you direct advice, it might be easier to give you an example of how one couple dealt with it. I draw upon the following excerpt from the fictional book *A notable or OK* by John Mellannamn.

To set the scene Frank and Holly are in their early 50s and have been in their relationship for about three years. Carol, who is best friends with Holly, is a similar age and has just started to date Trevor. Carol and Trevor have reached the stage where they have been to bed together, but there were problems in the erection maintenance department. In this scene Carol asks for advice from Holly on what to do. To help her, Holly recounts her own experience.

'I just don't think it's going to work out!' exclaimed Carol. 'We've been seeing each other for about three months now and we went to bed together for the first time last week. It was going really well, very romantic; although I think we were both a bit nervous...you know what it's like in your 50s and starting all over again. As soon as we were ready and I got the condom out, everything went downhill – literally! He said he couldn't do it and I don't know whether it was me or the bloody condom, or what. Maybe he just doesn't find me attractive in that way?'

'Rubbish! What's happened since then?' asked Holly.

'Not a lot really. We've talked about it a bit. He tells me he wants to do it and that things will be okay, but the circumstances have to be right. What am I going to do? I'd really like this to work, but I don't know how to go about it. I'm so full of anxiety right now. It takes a lot for a woman to take her clothes off at our age; there's so much self-doubt. What if he gets turned off again? What if he doesn't like what he sees?'

'I don't think people always appreciate the mutual anxiety when they go to bed together for the first time. They both want it, are ready for it, but there's so much going on in their minds that is never acknowledged' explained Holly.

'So what's the answer?' enquired Carol, opening their second bottle of Pinot Grigio.

'Well, there isn't a simple answer of course, but if I tell you what happened to us it might help ...just don't tell Frank!'

Both women settled themselves in the conservatory with their drinks and Holly began by reminding Carol how she and Frank had met through the internet. Like Carol and her new man, Holly and Frank were both divorcees in their early 50s. After a large gulp of wine, she explained that after a few weeks of dating Frank had anxieties in the bedroom.

'It's quite normal I reckon' explained Holly. 'We too went to bed together after a few weeks. Frank told me afterwards that he had that gorgeous thrill of excitement in his stomach but with the whole fear and dread thing, and it dominated his mind. It's a mental thing, not a physical one. It must be, because it's easy enough for them to get turned on watching something on the internet. Looking back I wish I'd had the courage to suggest to Frank that for the first time could we just go to bed and hold each other. But you don't say things like that because you're not always sure what the other person wants and expects. It's amazing that for something which is so intimate, we struggle to talk about it.'

'So things went wrong for you too?' asked Carol.

'Yes, it's not helped by those bloody condoms! There seems to come a point in a man's life when they just can't use them anymore. Frank laughs about this now, but it wasn't very funny at the time. He says that you wait for the right moment when you're at your stiffest, then you have to turn away and try to open a little packet, take out the condom, try and work out which way it unravels because it looks the same either way and then put it on yourself like you're bandaging a big toe. Any sensitive feeling you have is dulled by your dick effectively being covered in cling film. The moment's gone. That's why what happened to Trevor and what happened to Frank is quite common.'

'But you're okay now?'

'He still has his moments; I think most men do, but generally it's really good. The first time didn't go well but we were able to talk about it. I asked him how he felt about doing it with me and his reply was that he felt "sick". I asked him if it was really that bad. He said "To be honest, yes". It stemmed from not wanting to let me down. He likened it to being half way through a speech at a conference and then realising he hasn't got his trousers on. Naturally then, I wanted to know when he'd last had sex.'

'And when was it?'

'He'd been divorced for ten years and I knew he'd been in a couple of relationships since then. I think he was quite embarrassed; turns out he hadn't done it

123

since he was married – that's a long time for anyone. I asked him about the relationships since. Apparently it was a big thing for him and it got worse the more he tried. He said in the end it came between them, or he allowed it to come between them.'

'So what did you do?' asked Carol.

'To be honest the first thing you must do is talk about it. If you don't the problem never goes away. I'd read in *Cosmopolitan* about the advice couples get when they'd not had sex for a long time. So we talked about it. The first thing we agreed was that we would go to bed together, but we wouldn't have sex. I took the lead, but we determined between us what we could do and what we couldn't do. I understood his feelings about condoms, but as regards safe sex, as he'd not visited anywhere in the last ten years I felt he was a safe bet. So, although there was still anxiety it wouldn't be made worse by having to use condoms.'

'It wasn't just the use of condoms though?' asked Carol.

'No, it was a general fear on his part of not being able to do it.'

'So what sort of things did you do?' enquired Carol eagerly pouring another glass.

'Well, the next time we went to bed we just focused on getting close – kissing and just touching each other. We held hands and cuddled, but we didn't take our clothes off. I think he felt a little daft. Well, you do when you're starting again because it's what you did in your teens. I made sure that I never gave off any signals that I was just going through the motions. He said it was nice, and not having any pressure he did relax.'

'So that was the first time? What about the next time you got together?'

'The next time we got down to our undies. We touched each other, but nowhere that was still covered. I remember we stroked each other's skin and held each other close. Sometimes we'd hold each other and just talk. It was lovely.'

'How did he get on with that?'

'I could tell he was getting excited. When a man is down to his boxers he can't hide it, but it was all down to the fact that he knew we weren't going to have sex. There was no pressure. In fact, I think we did this a couple of times. At one point he wanted to go further, but I said no. It would have been too early.'

'So you really were taking your time?'

'Yes. The next time we were getting intimate in the bedroom we just wore our dressing gowns. It was in the evening and we had just one candle. I blew it out so it was completely dark. It was just like a film. We did get naked. I knelt beside him and put his hand on my neck and then moved it down to my breast and then left him to explore me on his own.'

'You're so confident, I'm not sure I could do that.'

'I think you've just got to go for it and take the lead; he'll appreciate it. Anyway, we touched each other in the dark, but there were still areas that were out of bounds. He did get very turned on, but it still wasn't the right time. I did tease him to be honest. I would brush the back of my hand along his cock. He groaned so I knew he wanted more of it.'

'And the next time?' Carol asked, a little wide-eyed.

'The next time we went a bit further. It was also evening. I'd set up three candles to light the room. I'd also brought up a bottle of red wine and two glasses. The plan was that we'd carry on touching, but this time we could touch everywhere and anywhere we liked. We could also use our lips and our tongues. We slowly undressed each other. I asked him to put a few droplets of the wine on my neck and shoulders and lick it off …but it all had to be done very slowly. It was great; he was so obedient – I think I could have asked for anything at that moment and he would have agreed. I then asked him to put some on my tummy and nipples and suck my skin dry. It was very sensual.'

'Wow! Where do you get these ideas from?'

'I occasionally read the odd erotic story.'

'I might need to read one myself. What happened next?' asked Carol with her mouth dry.

'It was now my turn so I dipped my finger in the wine and drizzled some over him. I then began to lick it all off. There were stains of red wine on his dick, which, as you can imagine, was quite stiff, so I licked and sucked it off – I'm taking about the red wine here by the way. It was then that I took his hand and put it between my thighs and showed him how to touch me.'

'Did you have sex then?'

'No. He said it was frustrating, but I think we did it a couple of sessions later. We made each other come in the meantime. The thing is that I knew that if we had done things too soon it could have made things worse. Anyway, men do like to be teased. It was mainly the fact that he knew we weren't going to actually have sex which really took all the pressure off.'

Mellannamn 2016, pp97-100

What comes from this is the need to help make your man feel totally at ease and therefore trust you. In a way it's part of his training. This may take quite a while, weeks even, because of the pressure he might put himself under. 'It is difficult for anyone to enjoy sex if they are fretting about their 'performance' and, needless to say, the more a person worries, the less likely they are to experience orgasm' (Godson 2011, p10). Therefore, you have to be strict about the rules. For example, go to bed together but state that you're not going to attempt sex even if it feels right. Be intimate, but clarify how far you both are going to go and where you're both allowed to touch. Sexually tease and turn each other on. Feel frustrated about not being allowed to go further. This might result in an erection because the pressure is taken away, but stick to the plan.

Each time you go to bed you might agree to go a little further. In this way the focus is more on the intimacy. It's only through these sessions and the sticking to the rules that he'll know whether he's capable. If you both try to hurry it then you can end up back at square one. Also, as I mention throughout this book, sex doesn't always have to involve penetration. In fact, you can still have a full and rich experience with just touching and stroking each other, as well as lots of fun. There's less anxiety, you don't have to worry so much about contraception and therefore it can alleviate any fears either of you may have about one of you getting pregnant. It's very intimate and there's less chance of catching something you can't spell.

Unfortunately, people perceive sex to be penetration, which often means that they don't attempt it and this can be a problem that can affect their whole relationship. As Godson (2011, p132) puts it 'once a couple stop having sex, even for a few months, they slip into "non-sexual relationship mode", where it becomes very difficult to initiate sex. They, in effect, become platonic partners in a conspiracy of silence'.

So, if you want to improve things in the bedroom where do you start and how can you go about it? There's only so much you can do as the trainer, the rest has got to come from him – with your guidance. Of course, it may be that what goes on outside the bedroom also needs to be addressed.

In the next couple of chapters, I direct my focus to your man and give him some ideas about his technique and his approach toward you. Have a read of them yourself first and if it's something you would like your man to consider then you need to work out a way of getting him to read it, as part of his training. If he likes what he reads he might end up reading the whole book.

# Chapter Eight

*Ideas for men in the bedroom*

In this chapter I cover
- What you want out of your relationship.
- The passion killer clothes.
- Making love to please your woman.
- How to find out what she likes without having to ask her.
- The female orgasm.

If you're a man and you're reading this chapter then chances are you are interested in your relationship, or it could be that you've just stumbled across it and are having a peak through. Perhaps you want some ideas on how to please your woman or how to improve your technique in the bedroom. Of course, it could be that you're just nosey and want to find out what she's been reading now, just in case there's a test coming your way.

*In a lot of relationships most couples don't realise that something isn't right*

## Your relationship

For most of us, when we start to have a relationship with a woman we're not really thinking long term. While we're with

129

them, we also have a tendency to keep a lookout in case there's something better out there, as if we're always ready to upgrade. But very often what we really need and what we are looking for is right in front of us; we've just let go a bit. Women generally are better at knowing what's best for us because we often place too much emphasis on the physical relationship.

In a lot of relationships, most couples don't realise that something isn't right. That's because changes are gradual over time and people tend to just adapt. But compare how you used to be together to how you are now. Do you still feel close or is the only kiss you get nowadays just from the dog? Do you have time for each other (no, not you and the dog, you and your partner)? Or, more importantly, do you want to have time together? You might find that most of your free time is taken up cleaning the car and caressing it fondly, giving it more attention than it deserves. You seem to do separate things now. Think about how it was in the beginning, how she used to look at you, how she used to crave being with you. Relationships do change and evolve, but ideally it should be in a deeper way.

If you've given it some thought (and I don't mean just since reading the last paragraph) and have noticed that things have become stale you need to question if you've contributed to this. Next you need to think about what you could do about it. This can be quite awkward. In fact, it's easier to do nothing at all, but then the situation never changes. Question yourself as to whether you would like to be closer to your partner or are just so set in your ways that it seems too much effort to change. Hopefully the answer is that you would prefer to have a joyful, closer relationship and you'd like your woman to be happy. If so, there are two places you can focus on. One is in the bedroom and the other, which I would say was probably more important at this stage and which I cover in the next chapter, is what you do outside the bedroom to make your woman want to be with you.

If it's the intimate physical side you would like to improve, but don't seem to be doing the right things, then read on. You'll find that it's about setting the scene, creating the right environment, and improving that technique of yours in order to develop the closeness between you.

## Before you get to the bedroom

What could be nicer than a woman wanting to go to bed with you, actually craving to make love with you? It's a nice feeling when someone sees you as desirable and you are the one responsible for the tingles she feels. We all want to be thought of as a great lover, don't we? Why would you want to have sex with someone who doesn't enjoy it with you? And don't say that you don't know whether she does or not because you don't discuss it anymore, you can sense it, surely! You've just chosen to ignore it and that's one reason why sex may be more of a ritual than as a sensual experience. It's so nice being able to turn someone on and pleasuring them. It's one of the few things in life that doesn't require any paperwork. Yet so many women see it as a chore or something that isn't quite as good as it used to be, or they just don't like it anymore. Whatever their reason they can't help the way they feel. But something must have happened to make them feel that way. So what is the point of making love to someone if they don't really enjoy it or feel particularly close to you?

The constant thought you need to have is to put your

woman first – this is essential. It means putting your own urges on hold and concentrating on her satisfaction. You need to be interested in pleasing her and you've got to show it in order to convince her. It means being patient and delaying your own satisfaction. Generally, most men are quite good at controlling and maintaining an erection. I'm convinced some have one for days on end. It shows that it can be trained because, in effect, it's our minds we're training. Also keep in mind that, to her, an erect penis is only sexy if it's an extension of you and your personality.

Making love should be like playing a piano concerto: building up gracefully and slowly and not just going for the same three chords all the time. You've got to build up your rhythm like Barry Manilow does in his songs (actually I'm not sure where that analogy came from, it just seemed right at the time). Yes, I know we like certain parts of the female anatomy more than others but you've got to take your time getting there. You've got to make her feel that it's all of her that you're making love to and every bit of her is as important as the next. If you go at it like a pneumatic drill and end up looking like a patient at the end of an episode of *Casualty* you really need to change your approach.

## Kissing

Was the last real kiss you had with her on your honeymoon? Women generally like kissing. I know it's quite a funny thing to do, two heads coming together joined by interlocking lips. We're never quite sure whether to keep our eyes open or not. If we leave them open and she opens her eyes at the same time it's a very weird moment, mainly because we can't talk with our mouth full. What other animal kisses? I'm sure there are some but mainly they rub noses or just smell each other's bottom. I'm not suggesting you do that by the way, although the rubbing of noses can be really sweet. For women, kissing is very important and the starting point to being close. Unfortunately, it's often the first thing that drifts away in a relationship, as men don't seem to like it as much. Maybe it's because it originated from mothers passing on pre-chewed food to weaning infants. Fortunately, we've all moved on from that now, so you're not going to find anything unexpected in your mouth afterward that you don't want.

In the early flourishes of attraction you probably couldn't put each other down, your lips were glued on to each other. You didn't even mind welcoming the visiting tongue, but then it moves on to the point where we're more worried about that loose filling or that it might be a bit unhygienic. Nowadays, you might miss the lips altogether and just go for a peck on the cheek. If so, you need to get back to interlocking lips, at least occasionally. You don't have to stick your tongue down her throat because that does seem a little bit embarrassing when you've been with someone quite a while, but you do need to kiss her. If she has bad breath then I'm afraid you're going to have to tell her as you would like her to tell you if all those pickled onions you eat at night was causing you bad breath. We generally like the opportunity of doing something about it.

## Clothes

As I mentioned in chapter five, we do tend to get attracted by sexy clothing: high heels, see-through nighties, stockings, suspenders and tassels or even uniforms. In other words, we revel at the idea of our women dressing up in the bedroom because it does arouse us. However, it tends not to have the same effect the other way around. If we dress up it looks more like a comedy turn, but that doesn't mean to say you can't think about how you look. Are you still wearing 'Y' fronts – white baggy ones …extra loose? They are not the most sexiest of garments. Do your feet get cold so you like to keep your socks on in bed? If you're in sexy mode, standing there with an erection ready for action with your socks on it is not a good look. Even worse is the combination of white baggy 'Y' fronts and socks (patterned ones seem to be worse for some reason). As for Long Johns, let's face it: they are all passion killers! Look in the mirror, would you find you sexy? In romantic films they never wear Long Johns or keep their socks on unless it's a comedy scene.

THAT REMINDS ME, I MUST DEFROST THAT CHICKEN.

There's no excuse for not thinking about your clothing. The great thing about the development of the gay scene is that you now have the freedom to wear really great clothes without anyone thinking you might be gay, if that's important to you. Think about it, if you started misbehaving with someone else you'd probably smarten yourself up for them. You'd want to impress someone new so why not your partner, especially if you want her to be more interested in you?

*We never ask questions about those things we feel we should know the answer.*

## In the bedroom

Sorry to let you down here, but you have to be aware that life isn't like what you see on your porn sites. Just like when you were little and cried at *Bambi*, you sort of realised at the time that it wasn't real. You, even at a very early age, could determine the difference between what was real and what wasn't. You now have to do it again. What you see on the Internet isn't reality and the vast majority of women are not represented there. When you see a hot looking shaven woman screaming out 'come on big boy, give it to me!' keep in mind that the next woman you go to bed with won't be like that. For a start most women generally don't orgasm just by penetration alone, and as for squirting, well honestly…

Internet porn is a production. It's like TV programmes that try to portray reality, but for the sake of drama they don't.

Good drama needs plenty of action and in soaps people tend to confront now and think later. Secrets always come out and characters always choose the most dramatic option. However, what makes for good soap operas does not always make for happy relationships. As compelling as it may be to act for the sake of action, this is not always the best way forward.

Marshall 2007, p152

This is why so many people react so inappropriately at times because they see it on TV and think it's normal human behaviour. It's not, and understanding the difference between the two is a part of adulthood.

The next thing you've got to do is find out what your woman likes in the bedroom. There's a simple way of doing this, ask her – actually, it's not that simple and there are two reasons for this:

1. From our point of view, when we feel we should already know something we generally don't like to ask.
2. Women can find it difficult to tell you what they like, especially when you've been together a long time and she's not told you before. Also, if a woman is inexperienced and nervous she feels that she shouldn't tell you.

With point number one, it's a bit like people who are not very good at their job. Very often this is down to two reasons: they don't know what their responsibilities are and/or they don't know what the standards expected of them are. In either of these cases they won't ask because it would make them feel exposed. We never ask questions about those things we feel we should know the answer. With point number two, it's difficult for a woman to tell you now because she doesn't want to make you feel that you've been doing it wrong all this time, or make you feel inadequate. As I mentioned previously, women are very good at protecting the male ego, that's why some fake orgasms – either that or they can't wait to get it over with. So it's going to be difficult for her. This means that you've got to try really hard to make her feel that she can be honest with you. This may take quite some time. If she feels that you're going to get upset, sulk or throw a tantrum, she won't feel it's worth it. These are all child-like behaviours as mentioned as part of the 'Adaptive Child' ego state (as mentioned in chapter four), which do not convey confidence in order for her to open up.

She has to feel secure that she can talk to you, that she can talk to the adult within you. For a start, it might be that she would like you to do something about your appearance. Your clothes may be doing nothing for her, that baggy tracksuit that you always wear or those jeans that when you bend over reveal that vertical smile of yours. It might even be the case that she can't stand you too hairy. If this is something that puts her off then you've got to buy a trimmer and do something about it. I see a lot of men when they go swimming with so much hair on their back that they look more like a descendant of a coconut. And when it starts becoming slimy and wet with all that sweat it's time to put the t-shirt back on – and keep it on! You might be too hairy under your 'Y' fronts, in which case, you might even have to think about starting to trim your balls to at least make them look presentable. I do advise caution here and that you use the correct setting with the protective guard on – any miscalculations at this stage and there won't be any future sex for you to worry about. It will take you a bit of practice, but if she likes it it's worth it. No one else has to know.

## Preparation

Foreplay is essential and the essence of love making for a woman, generally it's the bit you fast forward on your porn videos. Spending time on this is so important because it helps create the intimacy that then builds the excitement. The bedroom needs to be quiet, secluded and peaceful. If you always like to have the TV on while you make love get used to it being off. You, her and the TV – three's a crowd!

Set the scene by using soft lighting. You could even, dare I say it, use candles. Girls love candles, they find them romantic. A lot of women feel embarrassed about their own body even though you find it a real turn on, so subdued lighting can really help her feel more at ease. As time goes on and she feels more relaxed with you in bed you'll find that dimmed lighting may not be quite as important.

Make sure your phones are turned off or not within the vicinity. It can be very distracting wondering whether you're actually going to check who has just texted you. Have some soft music playing, make sure you're wearing your best boxers and put some aftershave on instead of that French furniture polish you usually use. I know it smells nice, but women can tell. However, don't wear too much that she has to struggle for oxygen.

## Making love

I mentioned in chapter seven how it can be a good thing to agree boundaries when you go to bed together. In other words, to ensure nothing goes wrong it might be an idea to state that you are not going to actually have sex and instead are just going lie together caressing each other. Having these guidelines takes pressure off and shifts the focus away from sex towards the feeling of being close, if this is what you want to achieve. If you intend to get physically close and perhaps make love, if you want to please your woman and make her feel nice and enjoy the experience, you need to focus on the sensual side. If you want some ideas how – then read the following excerpt as an example. Again I refer to the book *A notable or OK* by John Mallannamn.

Frank lay on the sofa at Holly's house reflecting on his relationship with her as he was waiting for her to return home. They had exchanged texts to each other earlier that day and as they had not seen each other for over a week both had indicated that they were feeling quite horny. Frank was just going through his mind about how he would like the evening to go. He wanted to make her feel special and so was plotting to pamper her.

He'd planned to compliment her and tell her how much he loved her. He would lead her to the bedroom which he had prepared with dimmed lighting. He would then sit her on the edge of the bed and kneel behind her. There he would gently kiss her neck and glide his fingers through her hair – she liked it when he did that. He'd progress to gently nibbling her neck and caressing her skin with his lips until he could sense her relaxing while massaging her shoulders at the same time.

After a while he envisioned gradually starting to undress her; just undoing a button now and again. He would then lay her down on the bed with her top unbuttoned and lie next to her. Leaning over her he'd pull down her loose top to expose her bare shoulders. He would then continue to kiss her and then slowly move to her tummy, but gently enough so that she could hardly feel him touching her with his lips. He wanted to cherish her as if she were delicate white China porcelain. After a while he would remove her top.

He knew that if she was wearing skinny jeans he wouldn't even attempt to remove them by himself;

not after the last time when he nearly knocked himself out. In his whole life he'd rarely ever been able to do it with any grace, especially if they were tight ones. When she's just wearing her bra and knickers he planned to stroke her skin gently as if he was hardly touching her. He would stroke her legs all the way down to her toes and then gradually work his way back up again. He'd then just run his fingers along the edges of her knickers. On the inside of her thigh he liked to tease her by doing gentle circular motions with the tips of his fingers as if mimicking making her come. He would then move his fingers to the other leg and do the same.

His idea then was to again start to kiss her neck and her shoulders, although he would allow his hand to move towards her thighs again. This time his fingers would creep their way inside her knickers but without them touching her. She liked this touch-teasing as she could anticipate the main event. This, he felt, built the intensity of the moment for both of them. Then he'd stop and glide his hands away and kiss her. He pictured Holly sitting up on the edge of the bed again as she had done so before. Kneeling behind her he'd undo her bra and just glide each strap down along her shoulders while he kissed her neck letting her bra fall off naturally. He wouldn't at this stage go grabbing her breasts as if they were going to fall off, but rather run his fingers from each shoulder down her chest along to her nipples, just firm enough for her to sense his touch. In a circular motion he would rub her nipples with the tips of his fingers and then cup her breasts in his hands.

He wanted her to hear in his voice how turned on this was making him feel.

He would then lie her on her tummy and with some lotion he would massage her for a while, caressing all parts of her body from her ankles to her neck, focusing mainly on her shoulders and back.

After a while Holly would roll over and while lying on her back next to him he would kiss her while stroking her body. Then, after a while, he would pull her knickers down …a little at a time, without taking them off. He felt this was a very sensual position to be in. Then he would focus on her thighs. He'd hover his hand over her between her legs and then tenderly land it. He would stroke her until he felt the tips of his fingers become damp as he slid them up and down moving towards her clitoris. He had become quite adept at finding that by now without her help; whereas, in the beginning he would invite Holly to guide him. He wouldn't go inside with his fingers unless he sensed that she wanted him to, but on occasions Holly would push his hand to show him what she wanted. He knew by now the pace she liked to be stroked. He could sense by the way she tensed her muscles and her breathing that he was doing it right and when she was building up. Occasionally he would tease her by stopping and moving his hand away only to return it a few seconds later. Then it was time to continue to undress her. He would then hold her hand in his and wrap her fingers closed. Then bringing her hand up to his mouth he would lick around her thumb and her index finger and then push his tongue into her palm with her fingers still closed. This was very sensual as it mimicked what he wanted to do to her next.

By now, with all this daydreaming and plotting, Frank couldn't wait for Holly to come home. He had a thrill in his stomach and a bulge in his trousers. His sole purpose was to satisfy Holly, but would only ever do things which she felt comfortable with. He'd learnt that by always putting her pleasure first the returns were great. He also had a better understanding, since meeting Holly, that sex didn't always have to be about penetration. It was about bringing her to orgasm in a way that she desired.

If they were to have intercourse he would always put a little cream or lubrication on himself first, which he always kept handy, as it just made the experience so much more pleasurable for both of them. He felt he could now sense her breathing becoming faster and deeper if he was doing it right, although he was always worried that it could be asthma.

Frank had realised that love making can often be more sensual when it was about mutual masturbation and that there should never be any rush to get his own needs satisfied. It was also important to Frank to always let Holly know from his responses that he liked what she was doing to him.

Tonight, to heighten the sensual nature of the evening, when Holly would make him climax with her hand he planned to simultaneously kiss her on the lips as he came. He'd done this before and found it to be very loving. Holly liked it because she felt close to him. He had to work on his timing and his positioning, but it was very erotic – although for some reason it always made his nose itch.

Frank felt things had progressed well. He'd gone through various stages in his sex life. He remembered, embarrassingly, from his young days shouting out 'Howay the lads' at the most inappropriate moment during sex and then to the point where he didn't feel that he'd ever be able to have sex ever again with another woman. Now he was lying there in anticipation of seeing his woman that evening and making love to her.

Mellannamn 2016, pp186-190

It is clear from this account that Holly had been instrumental in training Frank to be more conscious of her needs and it highlighted the gentleness a woman often craves. Frank had developed an awareness of how to create the right environment and not to rush lovemaking. He understood it was about Holly and her whole body, not just his favourite parts. As Jenner (2010, p39) identifies 'women have more erogenous zones than men and they like them to be used'.

An important point to make here is that the climax isn't the finale. When you have exploded and made a mess then generally, like most men, you're exhausted. It's an experience that consumes the whole body and one where, generally speaking, men don't feel the urge of doing again for quite some time (unless you're Christian Grey in *Fifty Shades*). Unfortunately for you, she may want to carry on. You may not feel like it, but you could make her come again. She will know if it's possible. Women's bodies are amazing and capable of so much more than ours.

When you have both finished make sure you kiss her tenderly. 'Women take much longer to come down from their sexual high than men do, which is why the period afterwards is so important' (Jenner 2010, p39). So, although you may have mentally detached yourself the least you need to do is lie together in each other's arms and cuddle. I know you want to check the half-time scores, but don't skip this important part of your lovemaking. Don't start picking up your *Gardener's monthly*, and definitely don't read her extracts from it, not yet anyway.

If your relationship is at the stage where you haven't made love for a long time, then don't try to rush it. It is something that needs to build up gradually. You need to be able to talk about it and have an agreement about how far you should both go, as discussed in chapter seven. Explore each other's bodies more, but stick to the rules and let the trust build between you.

This can also apply to those who are making love for the first time, a very disappointing event on most occasions. Boys often don't know what they're doing, nor do they have very good control. They tend to focus solely on the mechanics of the sex act and she's lucky if she gets get a full minute and a half. Their penis is a bit like a supermarket shopping trolley: it can have a mind of its own. One sneeze and it can be all over. Girls don't know what to expect and, because of the embarrassment of the situation, don't feel that they can talk about it, let alone explain what their own needs are.

One final point before I move on – if you really want to satisfy your woman, if you want to remove all pressure away from your own performance, then one of the most loving acts you can do is focus just on her pleasure without requiring anything in return. There are few men who do this and yet it can be a wonderful way of demonstrating your love and affection. A self-less act like this would be a sign that you want to put your partner first and that your feelings have no selfish intent behind them. If it's trust you want her to build up in you in the bedroom then this can be a great step towards it.

## Games

If you would really like to find out what your woman likes in bed but feel awkward about asking, there is a way. Make a bet with her over something where the winner receives a sexual forfeit. This means that the winner dictates everything that goes on in one session in the bedroom and the other has to obey, although you've got to let her win the bet. If you win, then how are you going to find out? Her winning and taking the forfeit means that you have to do everything she wants you to do to her. In this way she can feel more comfortable telling you what to do because you have to obey. However, if she asks you to dress up as a Roman slave and gets you to clean the whole house then she really hasn't got the hang of the game.

While she's using her forfeit then act as if you are her servant. It might take a while or a few goes to be comfortable with this, but it means that it gives her the chance of telling you, without any pressure, what she would like and it gives you the opportunity of glimpsing her fantasies. As with any sexual situation, for a woman to give herself to you she has to feel relaxed and that means she has to have trust in you. However, don't go quizzing her later in some sort of post-sex analysis session.

## The female orgasm

The female orgasm can be quite a daunting topic. For men, it's quite straight forward, you rub it long enough and hey presto! If you research this subject you can end up reading about all sorts of things including: clitoral orgasm, the G-spot orgasm, the multiple orgasm and the simultaneous orgasm. Apparently 75 per cent of men have an orgasm during sex compared with only 20 per cent of women. Keep in mind the words of Suzi Godson (2011, p30) – 'a fundamental design flaw means that the most sensitive part of our sexual anatomy happens to be outside, rather than inside, our vagina, and as a result many women need additional stimulation to reach the point of no return'. Therefore, you might need to ask for directions to find the clitoris because, as Godson (p56) continues '…few women can have a penetrative orgasm without any direct clitoral stimulation and although many women experience sensitivity and can orgasm, if the area known as the G-spot is stimulated, lots of women don't feel anything there at all'. Remember that there's no strict process to this because each woman is unique with a unique body. Your quest is to find out what her individual desires are and satisfy them. But always focus on the clitoris – never stray from the clitoris.

Now take a deep breath and relax. You need to think of other ideas to please your woman. Everything that goes on inside the bedroom is interrelated with what goes on outside it. The one complements the other. If you don't get the one right both areas suffer. In the next chapter, I go into what you can do to make her feel cherished and loved outside the bedroom. Find out what gifts are really worth, irrespective of price, and what else you could be doing to make her want you more.

# Chapter Nine

*Ideas for men outside the bedroom*

In this chapter I cover:
- What gifts say to her and what they are really worth.
- Little things that can mean a lot.
- Telling her you love her.
- Listening to her.
- Some final tips.

I suppose this chapter should have come before the previous one, because what you do in the bedroom is really determined by your relationship outside it. Making love is not going to be the main pastime, even if you do improve that technique of yours. Therefore, you need to work out what you can do to make your woman feel loved, feel cherished and for her to be impressed with you.

*Money doesn't make up for the fact that more important needs are not being met.*

## Gifts

Presents are always a good start, if you get it right. That sprocket set you bought her last Christmas didn't really have the desired effect you were hoping for, especially when it's been you who's been using it. Gifts are difficult to get right even when they are expected, such as birthdays and Christmas, but don't wait until then. Get her something when she least expects it. It doesn't have to be big, in fact bigger gifts can make you look a bit guilty, she'll think you've been up to something. It can be a single flake or one red rose. The message you want to get across is: 'I was thinking of you'.

Gray (1993) argues that it doesn't matter about the size of the gift as women have their own scoring system. Every gift is worth one point. You spend a lot of money on diamond earrings – one point. You buy her a car – one point. You buy her an inexpensive bunch of flowers – one point. You bring home a cake – one point. They all have equal value. It's the thought that counts, the one that says 'you're never out of my thoughts'. However, if you buy her a vacuum cleaner or an ironing board it's generally nil point. Practical gifts do not have the same worth.

Of course, this doesn't give you the excuse to go all-cheap on her, you still have to get it right. Men have made some awful mistakes in the past: the case of the young man who bought his 22-year-old girl-friend anti-wrinkle cream or the husband who bought his wife membership to Weight-watchers. And don't buy cheap perfume or anything from the pound shop. Also, be careful when buying clothes – too big a size can make her question your image of her, too small a size can make her think she's too fat. Stick to items like sexy underwear. This will, of course, mean that you'll have to go into lingerie shops and start groping through the underwear on display and wait for the young female shop assistant to ask you if you need any help – you're on your own there! My advice is look through her undies drawer, so you know the right size before you start this adventure.

Buying gifts when someone least expects is wonderful. However, it doesn't alleviate your responsibility to buy her a gift when she does expect it. My advice is don't forget birthdays and special days like anniversaries. These are the standards by which you must not fall below. It's easy to remember Christmas and Valentine's Day because they're advertised a lot. However, you need to go one step further. For example, sending her a card on the anniversary of someone's death who she was close to. She probably won't forget the date, but a card from you to say that you're thinking of her on this sad day will impress her greatly. It shows that you're sensing her emotions and you're concerned for how she may be feeling that day. It means, of course, that you will have to get a diary to put these anniversaries in, because once you start it's not something that you can just do for a while. You have got to be consistent.

Don't over-do the gift buying. You might be in a position where you are well off and/or you're always bringing her gifts. The assumption can sometimes be that she must know how much you love her because of all the gifts you shower her with. It doesn't make up for you not saying it. In relationships where money is not a prime concern, it can emphasise other aspects of the relationship which could be lacking. 'As a woman's financial needs are fulfilled she becomes more aware of her emotional needs' (Gray 1993, p129). Money doesn't make up for the fact that more important needs are not being met.

*Women like to see sensitivity.*

## Messages

When you're not buying her a gift, why not leave a note where she'll find it when you're not there? Leave it in the next chapter of her book, in her pocket, or in her socks drawer. However, make sure she'll be the only one who will find it. If her mother finds it thinking it's for her you might have to deal with all sorts of difficult situations, without even being aware of what's happened. Send her a text (no, not her mother), one to say you're missing her or how you're craving to be with her – the things you perhaps did when you first met. You don't always have to show your masculinity, women often prefer to see sensitivity. They often like to see a man who is not afraid to hold hands, kiss in public and pass them a tissue while they're watching something emotional on television – just before they need it. You might be sensitive and soft underneath, but that's not the bit that shows. Most of us have seen examples of how men can guard their emotions until their football team get relegated. Then it all comes flooding out. Women can wonder how a man can show so much emotion about a football team and not towards those who really matter.

Answer this question: when did you last tell her that you love her? ...And discount anything said when you've been making up after an argument – they don't count. If your answer was 'well, she knows that because I live with her', or 'I don't need to tell her because I married her', then you're just not getting it. Why is it so difficult to say? What is so uncomfortable about saying those words if that's how you feel? 'A man commonly makes the mistake of thinking that once he has met all of a woman's primary love needs, and she feels happy and secure, that she should know from then on that she is loved' (Gray 1993, p137). If you have said it to her recently, then question yourself as to whether you said it with any meaning. Sincerity can drift and it's hard to get back to the way it was before. It's difficult, and I know this works both ways, but no one said it was going to be easy. It's just that couples say it to each other in such a way that it seems like a throw-away comment. It's said in such a matter of fact way if they do say it at all, without any sincerity.

When did you last hold hands? When did you last hold hands in public? When did you last wash your hands? Women like clean hands and especially clean fingernails. Perhaps it's just a phase you're going through, but these phases become habit and then a way of life. It's so nice seeing an elderly couple in the twilight of their years walking together hand in hand. You do it when you're younger because you want to show affection to each other and you're not afraid to let the outside world know. So, why not now? Why should it be embarrassing to hold your partner's hand in public? Only you can answer that. Could you kiss her in public (even with your eyes shut)? Even if you don't like kissing at least pretend. If she knows you don't like kissing but you're making the effort she'll pretend that she doesn't know that you're pretending and then you can pretend that you don't know she's pretending not to know about you pretending. It's as simple as that!

## Getting closer

There is a difference between intimacy and the intimacy that leads to sex. It can often be misread by a woman so that when you want to touch her or kiss her in order to be close, she can often be guarded as she feels that it's leading to sex. You need to be patient here and let her confidence build up slowly that cuddling and touching are signs that you want to just be close and show your affection.

To start to get close you have to spend time together, just the two of you. If you want to impress her, have a meal together at the dining table and not while watching television. Cook a meal for her and let her relax, but don't do sausages because that's all you can do. Go on a picnic and take a bottle of champagne instead of going for the usual bar meal. Enjoy the simple pleasures like you did when you didn't have any money. If she's relaxing in the bath, why not bring her a glass of wine? Light some candles instead of her trying to relax with the bathroom light blazing in her eyes. Why not have a bath together? Of course, you'll have to make sure that you have the end with the taps sticking in your neck. Bring her breakfast in bed accompanied with a single flower in a vase. Spend an evening together just talking like you used to. Find out how she feels. Do you really know her? Then begin to find out. It will also mean an evening without the telly and without any sport. That's the good thing about PVRs as you can determine when you watch your programmes instead of TV schedules dictating your plans for the day. Why not dim the lights, put some music on, open a bottle of wine and sit and talk. Buy a couple of posh wine glasses just for the two of you. Under no circumstances start texting. In fact, turn your mobile phone off. The great thing about all this is that you don't have to apply for planning permission. You can do it all without anyone else's consent, not even her mother's.

*She'll admire and respect you for it*

# Listening

Listening is crucial. It means not talking or assuming you know what she is going to say. It means not watching the TV, reading the newspaper or your iPad at the same time that's she's talking to you. Listening is essential. It's important to a woman …it's important to us all.

If you practice listening your ability will increase and you'll find out all sorts of things. You can find out what she likes and what she doesn't like, what she wants from the relationship as well as what she dislikes – even about you. You can then do something about it. Of course, if she doesn't like your ears, you can't really do much about that unless you wear ear muffs. She might see you as being too hairy, for example. If that means you having to have your back shaved then do it, you can't blame her for that one. If you have children and you don't want any more and the subject of contraception comes up, you may have to do the gallant thing and volunteer yourself to have the snip. I know you don't like the thought of that. You're probably wincing right now as you're closing your legs. For most, the thought of an operation on our testicles fills us with dread, especially when it's out of choice. However, it might have to be done. She's always being messed around with or having to take the pill, so why not take that away from her. Do the honourable thing and have a vasectomy. She'll admire and respect you for it, even if it is only worth one point. She'll even let you explain the off-side rule to her again.

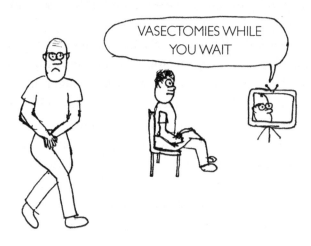

*...women like men who can make them laugh.*

## Other tips

Don't clean your ears, pick your skin or cut your toenails in her company. Always wash before sex (and after) and buy some nice aftershave – not cheap stuff where you can get a gallon for a fiver, I mean good stuff that will take away that 'just out of the hospital' smell you sometimes have. Compliment her now and again on how she looks. Also, keep in mind that women like men who can make them laugh. That's not so important for a man; they've got their mates to make them laugh. Also, women tend to dislike you flicking over channels while they're watching TV with you.

Lastly, and I feel I have to mention this, the old thing about not putting the toilet seat down. For some reason this is really significant to women. I don't know why either, but if it's important then don't question it or try to reason: just do it!

These little things can help make a difference in your relationship. However, you still need to know why women think differently and why they often have contrasting views about sex as well as about their own bodies. It is often related to what they have had to go through as women (very often at the hands of men). This I cover in the next chapter. Find out why she may feel more self-conscious about herself and how the lack of sensitivity she's received in the past can turn her off sex. Also, contrary to most popular fiction, I tell you what it's really like for most couples having sex for the first time.

# Chapter Ten

*Why women are different and why some don't like the*
*physical relationship*

In this chapter I cover:
- What makes women different
- Expectations from society.
- The lack of male sensitivity and sensuality.
- The female anatomy.
- The first time couples have sex.
- Women – the gatekeepers of sex and where men go.
- How women can question their own identity
- Sport on TV – it can be a man's world.

You might have noticed that women are different to men. First of all, they don't spit when they're having a pee. Why we do that, I'm not really sure. There must be something in our make-up that makes us feel the need to excrete from two places at the same time. Secondly, men don't go to the toilet in pairs. They're even uncomfortable sharing the same umbrella. And lastly (although I'm sure there are many more differences), all men seem to have a fascination about sex. However, not all women have that same interest. Some can take it or leave it, some did like it but have gone off it, particularly after the menopause, some go through phases, and some never liked it in the first place. So why is this and why are they so shy when it comes to their own bodies?

*…women think they are too fat to appear naked in*
*front of their partners*

## What makes women different?

One of the problems for women in society is the concept that they should all be as thin as models. It's continually in our faces: magazines, newspapers, billboards, TV programmes. We get bombarded with it all the time, and like all marketing its purpose is to create dissatisfaction with what we already have. Most of us don't look like that so we end up comparing ourselves to a minority of people instead of the majority – that's what we do in Westernised society. Not having the perfect body results in women feeling much more self-confident with their clothes on. However, in the bedroom it can have the opposite effect.

> …98 per cent of British women hate their bodies and that the average woman worries about her body once every 15 minutes. Indeed, a recent survey of 3,500 women by the bathroom company *Shuc*, revealed that a third of women think they are too fat to appear naked in front of their partners.
>
> Godson 2011, p125

Another factor that shapes women's image of sex is through romantic novels and films where, by the end, the man seems to know exactly how to treat his woman. They've been apart all the way through or been continuously arguing and misunderstanding each other, but then suddenly he's got it, without any training. In reality, these stories are nice but they're not helpful as they create a fantasy or a standard by which partners can be judged leading to disappointment (Skynner and Cleese 1993b).

Your experiences as a woman will probably be very different to what you've seen in films. You might have found that the men you've known seemed to have been a totally different species to those on the silver screen. They've thought differently and didn't know the first thing about developing a relationship; let alone satisfying a woman. You may have been (or are) in a relationship where your man has focused more on his own satisfaction, particularly in the bedroom, and this may have shaped your current attitude towards sex. 'Women, sadly, have suffered a great deal at the hands of men' (Jenner 2010, p259). Where was the sensual or the sensitivity; where was the foreplay? Where do you begin with putting a man right when he starts to feel amorous and certain parts of his anatomy are already heading in your direction? He just assumes the earth is going to move for you and that afterward you can just bask in the afterglow. In reality, it's probably that cobweb in the corner that's grabbed most of your attention.

A lot of women are brought up in such a way to not assert themselves and this is especially magnified at intimate times with their own needs. All the workings of the female body are often kept locked up inside as if it has to be all kept secret. The mechanics of the menstrual cycle and how everything comes together is not shared, let alone discussed. It's as if a woman should be ashamed of how her body works. That's one reason why they don't seem to fart. I think I was about twenty five before I realised women farted, and that was only because I saw the startled look on my dog's face when it was sitting on my auntie's lap and she let one slip out. And yet women can suffer from not just one type of air release, but two, in that vicinity. It can happen during or just after sex and has been called the 'vart' or a 'queef' – it's quite normal. If it coincides with flatulence it can steam up a man's glasses from three feet. It's all very natural and is only air trying to escape as it naturally likes to and yet it can be very embarrassing. There's no warning that it's going to happen; therefore, she has no control over the volume. She can't even let it slip out unnoticed. For a woman it can sound deafening. It's only when she feels totally at ease with her man that she accepts it and can laugh about it. If she's at this stage with her man he should take this as a compliment.

When men don't really know what they are doing in bed and women don't receive the gentle side of the sexual experience, it can leave a sense of something missing. Men tend to think women respond to the same stimulus and signals as they do which can alienate women even more. This is often why women fantasise about, and turn to, other women for relationships. Women often crave softness and tenderness in making love. If this is not fulfilled with a man they feel more likely to experience it with another woman, someone who understands and has the same needs – and who can blame them?

## The female anatomy

Another factor that can put women off sex is related to everything they have to deal with internally while on the couch at the clinic. Women have more check-ups than men. Men only go to the doctor as a last resort and it's hardly ever about their own genitals. It's usually 'man-flu' or some sort of rash they've discovered that can only be seen by holding two mirrors up at the same time.

Women have check-ups on a regular basis, that's probably why they live longer. Very often these check-ups examine very private and intimate parts of the body. That can't be very nice, especially when they're not always treated that sensitively (and this can be by other women too). However, they are better and usually braver at dealing with such things; whereas, men are much queasier. But if they've been fiddled with, poked and prodded, exposed in areas that are supposed to be associated with loving intimacy then it can hardly be surprising that they begin to disassociate that part of their anatomy as a destination that they want their man to travel to and explore. The thought of someone, who pays more attention to his own burps, thinking he knows what he's doing, is going to feel more like going for a medical examination. Some men are just not good with their hands, even after training. You've only got to look at the way he wraps up your Christmas present: it's more like something from a crime scene. It's got that 'wrapped up in the dark' look about it and he's never quite sure what's wrong with it *(bless!)*. If your man does happen to wrap presents really well chances are he gets a woman to do it for him.

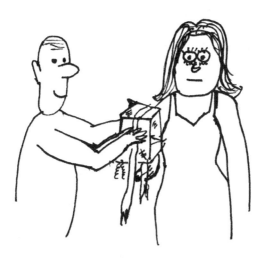

To you as a woman that little area between your legs can seem quite unsightly. Have you ever looked at yourself in the mirror and thought 'how on earth can anyone find that attractive?' Well, men do! And they think about it quite a lot. But it's understandable if you find it unusual or ugly that you think your man will too. This natural assumption contributes to feeling even more self-conscious. It's not as if you can compare yourself to your friends, and even if you wanted to I'm not sure how you would go about asking them.

This part of a woman is an amazing piece of machinery and design. It does all sorts of things with the most spectacular being a way out for a new-born the size of an inflated rugby ball. Giving birth to a baby through a hatch that doesn't seem to be big enough is quite astonishing. But then of course, sometimes it isn't big enough, so then there's the episiotomy where the midwife cuts the muscle that makes it easier for the baby to come out. So with all that going on down there it's little wonder women can be put off seeing that area as a headquarters for intimacy. No wonder they can be sensitive about being seen, let alone being touched.

*...was that it?' 'What the hell was all the fuss about'?*

## The first time

The first time a woman has sex it rarely turns out like Anatasia Steele's in *Fifty Shades of Grey*. Anatasia goes from virgin to full penetration and multiple orgasms in one very easy step. In reality, the first sexual experience for a woman, and often for a man, is awkward and clumsy with the after-thought being 'was that it?' 'What the hell was all the fuss about'? I expect you can remember what your first time was like – most of us can. I've not met anyone yet who said it went really well (not that I go about asking). A friend of mine said he was sick after he did it for the first time (mind you he had been drinking). The experience is often closer to the one found in the book *On Chesil Beach* by Ian McEwan where more things go wrong than right. A bad experience here can set the trend as to what women expect. Chances are that they may never find a man who really satisfies them. It must be very un-nerving for a young woman who may have had a sheltered up-bringing and who has been led to feel guilty about exploring how her own body works to find herself in bed with a naked man for the very first time. All of a sudden there's an erect penis coming her way that seems twice the size of the docking area and nothing has prepared her for it.

## Women – the gatekeepers of sex

As I mention earlier in the book, intimacy can drift away in a long-term relationship and having sex can evolve to the point where it becomes a ritual. It is then so easy to rely on the tried and trusted way of doing it, without ever really talking about it. Couples can then go years without having any sexual intimacy.

For other couples, women can very often become the gatekeepers of sex in the relationship. They determine when it is dished out (usually on his birthday) and how. They are often the one in control, which then becomes a way of life. However, if men go without it for long periods they often turn to other women and, strangely enough, men for casual sex.

They probably don't think of themselves as gay, but a high proportion of men will get some sort of sexual satisfaction in a very casual and fleeting way with another man.

For those of you who have been in a long-term relationship only to find out that he has turned gay, it's likely that he's always been gay. It's probably just that he's struggled and fought against it for quite some time, but finally admitted it to himself. There's really not much you can do in situations like these. The relationship is really at an end, although perversely he'll probably want to continue living with you and the kids to help conceal his sexual tendencies. Women, unfortunately, often have to accept this situation because they're not in a position to actually break free.

*A crisis is often the trigger for someone to question and search for their personal identity.*

## Identity as time goes on

Another thing that can happen to women is a loss of identity, especially when they have children. They play the role of a mother and as they are usually the ones who bring up the kids their career is put on hold. It can mean having to sacrifice wishes and desires for the sake of the family and any personal ambitions can bring feelings of guilt. Children become the main focus and the mother lives her life just for them. If the family are quite forceful then they often only see her as a mother, without individual needs and feelings. When the kids have grown up and left home it can be a time when she can end up questioning herself as to who she really is. She can go through years of not being heard or not being asked for her opinion; not being seen as an individual but as an extension of the family to focus on the needs of everyone else. The individuality can be lost.

It's strange that although parents use discipline to bring up their infants, it is often the children who become possessive and strict with the behaviour of their parents, especially as they get older. It's emphasised more, for example, when the mother expresses happiness and enjoyment even in her own home. They don't seem to like it and so they tell her off. This stifling of happiness can go to extremes, even in circumstances where there is a loss of a parent. The son or daughter is strongly against their widowed parent harbouring any thoughts of remarriage or even just having another relationship. This is, of course, totally selfish and out of order because it deprives someone of happiness. It's their own struggles in dealing with the situation which becomes more important than any consideration to the needs of the parent to actually move on.

A crisis is often the trigger for someone to question and search for their personal identity. It can be a time when they ask themselves 'who am I?' When this question is asked, it's often when people turn to counsellors or therapists, religion or even clairvoyance for the answer. Trying to come to terms with who they are can be very unnerving because getting back to the real person inside is difficult and painful. Some never reach it. In fact, there are many who put so many distractions in front of themselves just so that they don't have to confront who they really are. They can spend their whole lifetime ignoring their own issues. These distractions can include being ambitious in their career, always needing to be busy, always having people around them, portraying an image to gain others' approval, and even having children. It can often be closely related to having low self-esteem.

> It is often very difficult for people to identify the real self, and many people go through life convinced that the outer self, or self-concept, is the only reality they have. It sometimes takes a crisis to highlight the 'falseness' of the image which someone presents to the world. At times like this, a person may finally get in touch with the feelings, needs and ambitions which had previously been obscured.
>
> Hough 2014, pp147-148

When a crisis is forced upon us like a marriage break-up or a death, it can take a few years before we really feel ourselves again: we're no longer the person we thought we were. Until then we have less concern for the future as getting through the day ahead becomes our main challenge. In the worse phases, we can wake with a dread in our stomach of getting through to the evening when we can sleep again. Sometimes being asleep seems the only escape we have …that and fantasies.

In recapturing our identity, humanistic psychologist Carl Rogers (1967) talks about unconditional positive regard that we need from others in order to feel accepted. Unfortunately, some don't even have it towards themselves, even though they have it for others. They don't allow themselves anything less than perfection even as a mother. They create such high standards and personal expectations that when they don't reach them they see themselves as a failure, even when others don't. They are the ones who put pressure on themselves and won't tolerate anything less than faultlessness. Yet one of the hardest things we have to learn in life is to accept our own imperfections and ourselves.

Pressure can come in many forms. Even if a woman has a career, she usually has to be better than a man in order to be seen as equal. In society, there are different expectations of women and often their worse critics are other women. At the same time, she usually has to cope with everything expected of her in the home. It's often the case that she tends to do the jobs around the house that no one else will do. If she does a job just once it all of a sudden becomes her job.

## Sport and the TV

Women can easily get trapped in a male dominated world, even with the TV. They get conned into believing that the match on tonight is un-missable. Those of you who have a sports package will probably be aware that there's football on nearly every night of the week. There are all sorts of tournaments being shown all the time: world cups, domestic league and European competitions. And when they've run out of these matches, it's the under 21s, under 19s, over 35s 5-a-side, women's football, the over 90s – it's endless! With modern televised football we're now even in a situation whereby if we don't watch the match ourselves we end up watching someone who is. We watch panellists watching a match telling us what we're missing. And if the TV producers run out of football matches in this country they start showing those from other countries. Even when it's not the season it's the 'transfer season', or the 'build-up to the main event'. Sport can dominate a household. If it's not football it's cricket, rugby, Formula One, cycling, even fishing, and it all seem to be extended coverage. Soon it'll be cheese rolling and underwater hockey. If she doesn't like sport, and if the children are boys and the whole family like sport, she's got no chance.

With all this going on around them, with their constant self-assessment and a lack of confidence about their own bodies, it's little wonder that women need to have reminders that someone is thinking of them besides football. That's why they like to hear their partner tell them that they love them or that they're thinking of them. That's when they need their man to show signs of his feelings towards them before things can really begin to improve in the relationship.

# Chapter Eleven

## *Conclusion*

I hope you feel that it was worth investing your time reading this book. Perhaps it's got you thinking a bit differently or made you more aware of yourself as well as the relationship you're in (or contemplating being in). You might think that, after looking around at other couples, your relationship is quite 'normal', it's just that you don't really want 'normal'. You might have concluded that you have separateness but very little togetherness and you're now considering what to do about it. There could be decisions you now need to make.

> To live the life you want, you need to know what you want. Being effective in the world means producing the results you choose. The first step is to choose. If you do not, there are plenty of people willing to choose for you.
>
> O'Connor and Seymour 1993, p10

The intention here was to create something readable that you could relate to, without any exercises and tasks to complete. Like anything, you decide what you take from it and what you feel you don't need. You'll have found things that you agree with and those that you don't. However, if you are interested in the concepts I've covered and would like to find out more then I recommend reading *Men are from Mars, Women are from Venus* by John Gray, *The Road Less Travelled* by M.Scott Peck, and *Families and How to Survive Them* by Robin Skynner and John Cleese.

*When couples get married there's nothing that says that they have to live with each other all the time.*

You might have read this book because you wanted to develop your own awareness so that you can help others. As I mentioned in the first chapter, in order to talk intimately with someone we need to feel confident in them, someone who we can trust and who will really listen to us. If your aim was to help understand yourself and your relationship better but have found that you still don't know how you feel then think about keeping a journal. Write down your thoughts at random and then put the journal away. As the weeks pass you'll see the direction you're going. The problem with keeping our thoughts locked in our mind is that they swirl around and evolve and we can't remember how we felt about things before. Going back to read it after a few weeks often enlightens us as to the way our thinking has moved on. All this contemplation is hard; it can wear us down because it's all to do with self-discovery and accepting who we are. 'We cannot move away from what we are, until we thoroughly *accept* what we are. Then change seems to come about almost unnoticed' (Rogers 1967, p17).

Most of us would like to have a partner in our lives, but we may have to admit that living with someone and seeing them every day may not be the best thing for our relationship. So many couples live together but apart, whereas the relationship would be much closer if they lived apart but together – there's a big difference there. It might be better to have this healthy love of togetherness and separateness by actually living apart – separately together. When couples get married, there's nothing that says that they have to live with each other all the time. For example, you could just be together at the weekends and perhaps one evening during the week. This way you can look forward to being with each other and not take your time together for granted. You can then watch what you like on TV, do your chores when you want, cater for yourself and not worry about someone else and what time they come home. Just imagine having the remote control all to yourself. You then get all the best bits of a relationship. There's nothing wrong with being independent, you can still be great lovers. Some in relationships crave time on their own, but can't voice it in case their partner sees it as a threat – not wanting to be with them.

For some of you who have been together for a long time, it might be that you have scars that run too deep and therefore have little, or no, inclination to improve your relationship. It might be that you are focusing, not on your relationship but, rather, on yourself and your life. Alternatively, you might have found that the man you have, with all his faults that infuriate you, the man that there's no toilet he can't miss standing up, is really the one you would like to be close to again.

*His sex education has probably been quite poor, so don't be the one who suffers for it.*

Real life is out there; it's in you. It's rarely found in films. I mentioned in the introductory chapter that deep down we invariably know what we should be doing and what the right things are in our lives; we just choose not to go down that road because facing them means having to examine ourselves. It's much easier to find someone to blame. However, we should be focusing on moving on and progressing. In the end, *you* is all you've really got and this is who you might have been searching for. In your quest you may have learnt lots of new things. Unfortunately, with learning you can't go back to the way you thought before. Self-discovery and awareness are not always pleasurable experiences, especially at the time.

In summarising the book in reverse order, in Part Two I talked about how men think, even during sex. This might have been the main reason why you read the book, you wanted to understand the workings of their minds in comparison to your own. I hope it didn't put you off your man. And I really hope you're not now cross-examining him. It might be that you now think he's more normal than you originally thought; whereas, before you just thought he was a bit kinky (as my girlfriend did with me).

One of the most important principles I've tried to get across is for you to understand your own needs first. If you don't know what they are you've less chance of your partner working them out and being able to satisfy you, especially in the bedroom. In chapter six, I wanted you to be aware of these because you have got to take the lead in guiding your man. His sex education has probably been quite poor, so don't be the one who suffers for it. What I have covered was more sex education as a precursor to you being the trainer. If you're still not sure what the difference is between education and training then just answer this question: would you prefer your daughter to receive sex education or sex training? In many of the situations you find yourself in it's more than likely it's going to be you who needs to direct him. The time for sex education has passed; it's time for training.

*No one can change the past, but they can take something from it for the future ...*

Although this book is written essentially for women it is beneficial for men too. In chapters eight and nine, I directed my focus to them. I thought that if I wrote material solely for men they probably wouldn't read it, but they might read a little bit of the book you're reading – especially if they know there are bits about sex in it.

Apart from the main recommendation that most couples should live separately together, from a practical perspective I see the book as trying to convey three important messages, the first one being about identifying your own needs initially and then training your man. The second is aimed at men to respect and have more empathy towards their partner, treating her with consideration, cherishing her and treating her like a woman, inside and outside the bedroom. It's only then that the relationship can develop. It's only then that the love you have can go deeper and reach a closeness that can rarely be gained from a fling or any other short relationship.

I've also tried to give you an understanding of why your man might not want sex (chapter seven). Alternatively, if he reads the book he might begin to see why perhaps you've gone off it. Reading chapter ten can be a starting point for him in understanding how you feel and what you may have been through.

If there was a third important message in the book it was to give the reader more of an awareness of themselves which will help to develop an understanding of their relationship and why it can break down. In chapter two, I showed how the ideals and expectations derived from novels and films can make us feel disenchanted with what we have. Here I tried to define the difference between a healthy love that can last, and an unhealthy love which is based on dependency. However, with any relationship, if our needs are neglected it can often mean we take them to someone else who we feel understands them. Therefore, in chapter three, I tried to give a non-judgemental perspective of why people seek intimacy with someone other than their partner.

There are approximately 3.4 billion men in the world, so you may be thinking how come you ended up with the one you've got. In chapter four, I offered an answer by outlining how we come to choose our partner. At the same time, I wanted the reader to be more aware of their own behaviours and where they stem from as these have a direct influence on our personality, as well as the choices we make in life. It also determines how effective or ineffective we are at communicating.

One of the intentions of the book was to help those in relationships understand them more whether they be couples who have been together for a long time, recently married, or even those just starting out. I've covered some deep stuff and tried to balance it out with a lighter side. I've added humour to soften any intensity that might come from the contents, but I've also done this to help you relate to the examples I give and hopefully for you to see the funny side of the situations you might find yourself in.

I've tried not to give direct advice, although it may not have always come across like that. There will be some who wanted this, but telling you specifically what you should and shouldn't do would not work because every relationship is different and every person is unique. What works for one would not be appropriate for another. The book is more about giving you ideas and for you to find a starting point to help you to move forward. However, if you are desperate and really would prefer some direct advice then here it is:

1. Don't leave your lip salve in the same draw as your *Pritstick*.
2. Never go to sleep without sorting out issues with your partner.

The second piece of advice is probably more important in a relationship than the first one, although I have made that mistake myself with the *Pritstick* in the past. Imagine if your partner died and your last moment together was you being in the 'Adaptive Child' ego state, angry with him or not talking – you'd have to live with that forever. Sort out your issues before you sleep. There's nothing worse than waking up the following morning and starting the conversation with: '*And* another thing…'

*You really have to understand yourself first before you can share yourself with someone else.*

To be honest, all the ideas I've included in this book are not revolutionary, especially the one about the *Pritstick*. I'm not going to be awarded the Nobel Peace prize even if it does help couples with their relationship or prevents their lips sticking together. It does take two to make a relationship work and both have got to want it to work. Reading this is the first step. Unfortunately, if you can't influence him to read the book, then the onus is on you to get things rolling and you can't do that until you perceive what your own needs are, understand how he thinks, and realise what's going on in your relationship.

Relationships are important. Like us as individuals they are at the centre of most things we do, that's why we search endlessly for the right one or try to recapture what we once had. It's so nice sharing our life with someone, but it's also important that we feel the desire to be with them. That's why living apart can bring so many benefits. I'm convinced that more relationships would have worked out better had they not lived together.

Relationships are a normal part of our make-up and that's why I've talked about marriage, but emphasised the need to make sure it's the right thing to do. I've questioned why people do get married. I've done this just to make sure it's not something that's rushed into without thinking of what's involved and what it's really all about. It's an important decision and not one that should be taken lightly. Remember the question: how do you know how you feel?

If you take one message from this book, then perhaps it should be this: you really have to understand yourself first before you can share yourself with someone else. It's only then that a partnership can really work; this, I feel, is a really important concept to understand. For many of us, we don't find out about ourselves, or who we are, until many years into a marriage when we're much older, and as by then we have a family it all becomes more complicated. It's often a crisis that makes us question ourselves about what we really want. That's why so many marriages fall along the wayside. But don't misunderstand me; I'm not against marriage. In fact it can be quite wonderful sharing your life with someone and having someone always there to support you. It's a marvellous invention ...but so is the bicycle repair kit.

IN THE END THE TWO OF THEM DECIDED THAT THEY DID LOVE EACH OTHER, SO THEY LOWERED THEIR EXPECTATIONS, AGREED TO LIVE SEPERATELY AND SEE EACH OTHER REGULARLY. THEY LIVED REASONABLY CONTENDED EVER AFTER.

# List of References

Andreas, S. and Faulkner, C. (1996). *NLP: The New Technology of Achievement.* London, Nicholas Brealey, London

Berne, E. (1964) *Games People Play.* Random House, Toronto

Godson, S. (2011) *Sex Counsel.* Cassell, London

Gray, J. (1993) *Men are from Mars, Women are from Venus.* Thorsons, London

Harris, T. (1973) *I'm OK – You're OK.* Pan Books, London

Hornby, N. (2000) *High Fidelity.* Penguin, London

Hough, M. (2014) *Counselling Skills and Theory.* 4th Edition. Hodder Education, Italy

James, E.L. (2012) *Fifty Shades of Grey.* Arrow books, London

Jenner, P. (2010) *Have Great Sex.* Hodder Education, Oxon

Larkin, P. (1999) *High Windows.* Faber and Faber Ltd, London

Lodge, D. (1992) *Paradise News.* Penguin, London

Marshall, A.G. (2007) *I love you but I'm not in love with you. Seven steps to saving your relationship.* Bloomsbury, London

Laertius, D. (2014) *The Lives and Opinions of Eminent Philosophers.* CreateSpace Independent Publishing Platform

Maslow, A.H. (1970) *Motivation and Personality.* 3rd Edition. Harper & Row, New York

McEwan, I. (2008) *On Chesil Beach.* Vintage Books, London

Mellannamn, J. (2016) *A Notable or OK.* Mystic Utopia, Birmingham

Moxon, D. (2001) *Human Relationships.* Heinemann, Oxford

Myers, D.G. (1989) *Psychology.* 2nd Edition. Worth, New York

O'Connor, J. and Seymour, J. (1993) *Introducing NLP.* Aquarian Press, London

Pile, S. (1980) *The Book of Heroic Failures.* First Futura Publications, London

Rogers, C.R. (1967) *On Becoming a Person.* Constable and Company Ltd, London

Russell, W. (1989) *Shirley Valentine.* Paramount Pictures, UK

Scott Peck, M. (1990) *The Road Less Travelled.* Arrow Books, London

Skynner, R. and Cleese, J. (1993a) *Families and How to Survive Them.* 3rd Edition. Cedar, London

Skynner, R. and Cleese, J. (1993b) *Life and How to Survive it.* Methuen, London